New ideas for
CREATIVE
PRAYER

by
Judith Merrell

Scripture Union, 207–209 Queensway, Bletchley, MK2 2EB, England.

© Judith Merrell, 2001

ISBN 1 85999 589 6

Unless otherwise stated, Bible verses quoted before each prayer activity have been taken from the Good News Bible, published by the Bible Societies/HarperCollins Publishers Ltd., UK © American Bible Society 1992, used with permission.
Abbreviations: (CEV) Contemporary English Version, (NIV) New International Version.

British Library Cataloguing-in-Publication Data
A catalogue record for this book is available from the British Library.

Cover design: 3T Creative
Internal design: 3T Creative
Illustrations: Wendy Hobbs

Printed and bound in Great Britain by
Creative Print and Design (Wales) Ebbw Vale.

Scripture Union:
We are an international Christian charity working with churches in more than 130 countries providing resources to bring the good news about Jesus Christ to children, young people and families – and to encourage them to develop spiritually through the Bible and prayer.

As well as our network of volunteers, staff and associates who run holidays, church-based events and school Christian groups, we produce a wide range of publications and support those who use our resources through training programmes.

CONTENTS

KEY TO SYMBOLS:

To help you assess the suitability of each prayer for use with your own group, the following symbols have been used.

 can easily be used or adapted for use with three- to five-year-olds.

suitable for a mixed age group or all-age service.

 craft equipment required.

can be used as part of a five-minute all-age talk.

 suitable for use with six to eleven-year-olds.

INTRODUCTION

I'll always be indebted to my parents for teaching me to pray at bedtime.

As I was growing up they would always say prayers, with my sister and me, straight after our bedtime story. It was a few moments of quality time when they heard a little more about some of the good and bad things that had happened during our day. My mother still quotes the time when she heard me, aged about five, say, 'Oh! And by the way God, thanks for keeping me quiet in assembly!' That was the moment when she first realised that my poor teacher needed her prayers, as she had a lot to contend with!

I am now trying to bring up my own two small children with a similar bedtime routine. It's not always easy, as they find it difficult to understand why they should talk to someone that they can't see or hear. One night, in a bid to gain my son's concentration, I insisted that he closed his eyes and put his hands together. 'Why?' he asked. 'Is God in between my fingers?' Many of the prayers in this book do not require children to sit with their 'hands together and eyes closed'; instead they take a variety of creative approaches. There are prayers for your group to write, draw and make, prayers to join in, prayers with accompanying actions, prayers to think about and discuss, prayers that require participation. All too often, church leaders and Sunday group helpers say prayers on behalf of the rest of the group. When this happens, many children find it hard to keep their attention from wandering. Others spend the time trying to wink at anyone else who still has their eyes open! The following 101 prayers invite the whole group to get involved and, where children and young people participate, their concentration often follows!

PRAYERS TO JOIN IN

In church and Sunday groups, prayers are frequently said by a leader, on behalf of everyone else. This is a great opportunity for youngsters to take a break from concentrating and quietly (or not so quietly) think their own thoughts! Often the prayers go right over their heads while they peer at the world around them through the gap in their interlaced fingers, and attempt to catch the eye of anyone else with their eyes open.

Sorry, Lord.

We really want to say.... thank you, Lord.

One way to encourage children to participate is to give them the chance to join in with a response. In this following section, many of the prayers can be read by a leader, with the group joining in with the response (*shown in italics*). It is always a good idea to practise the response in advance and to give a clear lead by repeating the words loudly yourself. For younger children, there are also one or two prayers with accompanying actions, and for early readers there are some short prayers to read aloud together.

Thank you, Jesus, that you died for me.

Hallelujah!

Another way to enable youngsters to participate fully in the prayers is to invite them to contribute items to pray about. In this way the whole group or congregation can 'own' the prayers that are said, so they are not merely something that is said on their behalf.

Amen!

1. PRAYER STARTER

'Lord, teach us to pray...' Luke 11:1

YOU WILL NEED: cards with statements listed below; three paperclips per person.

Write out the following ten statements on individual pieces of card and fix them up around your meeting room:

Prayers are boring because they go on and on.
Most prayers include too many long words.
I never know what to pray about.
Talking to God is just like talking to a friend.
Sometimes I forget to pray.
It's good to pray every day.
I talk to God about everything.
I always pray in times of trouble.
It's best to pray in church.
I only talk to God about the mega-important issues.

Give each child three paperclips and ask them to walk around, reading the cards, and then fix their paperclips onto the three statements that they agree with most strongly. Bring the children back together to count up the votes and comment on the group's collective feelings. Point out that even the disciples found it hard to pray, and they had to ask Jesus to help them.

Jesus wants us to talk to him regularly, just like we talk to our friends. He doesn't want us to use any special language or long words when we talk to him, and we don't have to pray at great length. We don't even need to pray out loud if we don't want to. All

8

we need to do is think in our heads what we want to say to Jesus, and he hears it. Prayer is amazing and it's our own special way of keeping in touch with Jesus and asking him to be involved with every aspect of our lives, big or small. REMEMBER…

Anyone can pray about Anything, Any time, Anywhere!

Finish with a prayer asking God to help each group member to make an opportunity to pray each day during the coming week. Pray that God will also help each person to find the right words to express their personal feelings, worries, concerns, love and appreciation.

2. AN OPENING PRAYER

'Come to worship him with thankful hearts and songs of praise.' Psalm 95:2 CEV

As we gather together,
Lord, help us to concentrate on you.
As we put aside the things that distract us,
Lord, help us to concentrate on you.
As we leave behind the things that worry us,
Lord, help us to concentrate on you.
As we forget about ourselves,
Lord, help us to concentrate on you.
As we worship you with songs of praise,
Lord, help us to concentrate on you.
As we listen to stories from your Word,
Lord, help us to concentrate on you.
As we hear your teaching,
Lord, help us to concentrate on you.

3. WASH AWAY WRONGDOING

'Wash me clean from all my sin and guilt.' Psalm 51:2 CEV

YOU WILL NEED: OHP; water-soluble pens; water; cloth.

Ask your group to help you make a list of all the things that we do that make God feel sad. Use a water-soluble overhead projector (OHP) pen to write all their ideas onto acetate. Once the list is complete, weave all their suggestions into a response prayer something like the following:

For all the times we make you feel sad
We want to say… Sorry, Lord!
For the times when we lie and cheat
We want to say… Sorry, Lord!
For the times when we are bad-tempered and grumpy
We want to say… Sorry, Lord!
For the times when we are rude or naughty
We want to say… Sorry, Lord!
For the times when we deliberately disobey
We want to say… Sorry, Lord!
For the times when we are selfish or unkind
We want to say… Sorry, Lord!
For all the wrong things we do
We want to say… Sorry, Lord!
Amen.

When the prayer is over, sprinkle one or two drops of water onto the acetate and watch the water dissolve the ink. Next, use a cloth to wipe the whole acetate clean to illustrate that when we say sorry to God he forgives us and wipes away our wrongdoing, giving us the opportunity to make a fresh, clean start.

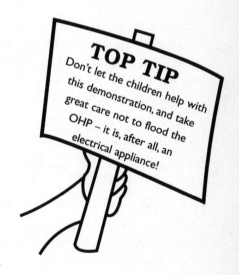

TOP TIP
Don't let the children help with this demonstration, and take great care not to flood the OHP – it is, after all, an electrical appliance!

4. GOD LOOKS ON THE INSIDE

'Man looks at the outward appearance, but I look at the heart.'
1 Samuel 16:7

YOU WILL NEED: a selection of lunchboxes/bags, including one that is sparkling clean on the outside but very dirty inside; bowl of soapy water; washing-up brush.

Explain to your group that you are going to make a packed lunch and that you need a box that is just right. Look at all the lunchboxes available and comment on their size and various merits. Eventually choose the one that is dirty on the inside. (Adding a few mouldy crusts and an old apple core would really illustrate the point well!) Look shocked and horrified when you open the box and point out that from its external appearance there was no way of knowing that this lunchbox was dirty, unhygienic and a sure carrier of food poisoning and numerous other bugs!

Go on to explain that people are just the same. On the outside we all look like fairly presentable, acceptable human beings; only God knows exactly what we are like inside. Ask the group to help you list some of the bad qualities that might spoil a person inwardly; for example, selfishness, pride, hatred, envy, lies. Try to think of some specific examples that fit the age and circumstances of your group. Ask the group to join you in saying a 'sorry' prayer for all these wrong things. Practise the italicised response before you start.

For the times when we are selfish and think only of ourselves,
We really want to say, 'Sorry, Lord!'
For the times when we are proud and think that we're better than others,
We really want to say, 'Sorry, Lord!'
For the times when we get cross or impatient and hate our friends and family,
We really want to say, 'Sorry, Lord!'
For the times when we are envious and not content with the good things we have,
We really want to say, 'Sorry, Lord!'
For the times when we lie to impress others or to get out of trouble,
We really want to say, 'Sorry, Lord!'
Lord, wash us clean of all these wrong thoughts and feelings that spoil our lives. Help us to be clean on the inside so that our hearts and minds are pleasing to you. Amen.

When you have finished the prayer, wash up the lunchbox to demonstrate that, when we say sorry to him, God always gives us a fresh, clean start.

5. CLOSE BESIDE US

'You are all round me on every side; you protect me with your power.' Psalm 139:5

Invite the group to use both hands to point in front of them, behind them and to the sides during the relevant sections of this prayer. In the last two lines they should wrap their arms around their body and hug themselves.

Jesus is before us
Preparing the way.
Jesus is behind us
Helping us, come what may.
Jesus is beside us
He's here with us today.
Jesus is always with us
Every hour of every day.

6. STRONG ROOTS

'Keep your roots deep in him, build your lives on him, and become stronger in your faith, as you were taught.' Colossians 2:7

YOU WILL NEED: a punnet of cress; a jug of water.

Buy a punnet of cress so that you can ease it out of the plastic tub and show your group its root structure. Explain that a plant's roots are vital for drawing up water and nutrients from the soil. Without strong roots the cress would wilt and die. The Bible tells us that we should sink our roots into Jesus, building our lives on him and thus growing strong in our faith. If our life is not rooted in Jesus, our Christian faith will wilt and die. Regular prayer, like regular watering, can help us to grow strong roots.

TOP TIP

Take in a punnet of cress that has wilted slightly. Water the cress and watch how it draws up the water and gradually returns to an upright position. Try this out at home first.

Finish by asking the group to repeat the following prayer after you, phrase by phrase. Alternatively, write out the words on an OHP acetate for everyone to read aloud.

Please help us to grow stronger in our faith every day.
Help us to root our lives in you and grow closer to you.
Thank-you for the power and strength that you give us.
Amen.

7. GOD IS ALWAYS WITH US

'For God has said, "I will never leave
you; I will never abandon you."'
Hebrews 13:5

Wherever we are, every hour of the day
Whether we're at work or busy at play
God is always with us.
When we're feeling happy or perhaps a bit sad
During the good times and the bad
God is always with us.
At school or at home
With friends or on our own
God is always with us.
Morning, noon and night, every single day
Weekdays, special days, high days and holidays
God is always with us.
Thank-you, God, that you never leave us.

8. GOD CARES ABOUT EACH ONE OF US

'Why do we humans mean anything to you, our Lord? Why do you care about us?' Psalm 144:3 CEV

Whether we're big or small,
Whether we're short or tall,
God cares about each one of us.
Whether we're slow or fast,
Whether we're first or last,
God cares about each one of us.
Whether we're quiet or like to shout,
Whether we prefer to stay home or go out,
God cares about each one of us.
Whether we're dark or fair,
Whether we have curly or straight hair,
God cares about each one of us.
No two people are quite the same,
But God knows each of his children by name and...
God cares about each one of us.

9. CREATION PRAISE

(3-5) (6-11)

'All creation, come and praise the name of the Lord.' Psalm 148:13 CEV

YOU WILL NEED: craft equipment (optional).

Teach your group the prayer below and invite them to join in with the response 'Come and praise the Lord!'. Then, ask the youngsters to contribute a few more lines of their own, or encourage them to write a new prayer using a similar response. Use Psalms 148 and 150 as inspiration.

If time allows, write the prayer in the middle of a large sheet of paper, then hand out circles of paper and ask each child to illustrate one line of the prayer. Stick the circles all around the prayer to make one big prayer poster.

Purring cats and barking dogs
Come and praise the Lord!

Laughing ducks and croaking frogs
Come and praise the Lord!

Rumbling storms and soft showers
Come and praise the Lord!

Rustling leaves and whispering flowers
Come and praise the Lord!

Singing birds and buzzing bees
Come and praise the Lord!

Lapping waves and crashing seas
Come and praise the Lord!

Let everything that has breath praise the Lord.

10. THE POWER OF PRAYER

'...his faith filled him with power, and he gave praise to God.' Romans 4:20

YOU WILL NEED: a clockwork or battery operated toy.

Wind up your clockwork toy and let the group time how long it continues to work. Ask the group to guess in advance how long it might last. Award a sweet to the child whose guess comes closest. Observe how the toy gradually winds down and runs out of steam. It's a bit like that in our Christian lives – without prayer, teaching and fellowship we run out of energy and wind down.

If you do not have a clockwork toy use a battery operated one, but remove the battery beforehand. Ask the group to work out why it doesn't work, and demonstrate the difference once the battery has been inserted. Explain that prayer, teaching and fellowship help to fuel our Christian lives just as the battery powers the toy.

(With thanks to Ali Matchett.)

Conclude with the prayer below, but take a moment to practise the response first.

Please help us to pray regularly,
Father God, give us your strength and power.
Please help us to read and understand your Word,
Father God, give us your strength and power.
Please help us to follow your way,
Father God, give us your strength and power.
Please help us to draw closer to you,
Father God, give us your strength and power.
Please help us to tell others about your love,
Father God, give us your strength and power.
In every part of our Christian life,
Father God, give us your strength and power.

11. BE FILLED WITH THE SPIRIT

'For the Spirit that God has given us does not make us timid; instead, his Spirit fills us with power, love and self-control.' 2 Timothy 1:7

YOU WILL NEED: a jug of water; a bowl; a plastic or polystyrene beaker; a knitting needle or similar.

Explain to your group that in some ways the beaker is just like us. (Fill the beaker with water.) We ask God to fill us with his Spirit and he does so. Sometimes, because we're only human and far from perfect we spring a leak. (Make a hole in the base of the cup so that the water drips through gently.) Since we're using God's Spirit to strengthen and empower us we need to pray that God will refill, refresh and refuel us again and again. Conclude with the following response prayer based on Galatians 5:22,23.

Father, we really need your love in our lives,
Lord God, please fill us with your Holy Spirit.
We really need your joy in our lives,
Lord God, please fill us with your Holy Spirit.
We really need your peace in our lives,
Lord God, please fill us with your Holy Spirit.
We really need your patience in our lives,
Lord God, please fill us with your Holy Spirit.
We really need your kindness in our lives,
Lord God, please fill us with your Holy Spirit.
We really need your goodness in our lives,
Lord God, please fill us with your Holy Spirit.
We really need great faithfulness in our lives,
Lord God, please fill us with your Holy Spirit.
We really need quiet humility in our lives,
Lord God, please fill us with your Holy Spirit.
We really need strong self-control in our lives,
Lord God, please fill us with your Holy Spirit.
We really need the strength and power of your Spirit in every aspect of our lives,
Lord God, please fill us with your Holy Spirit.

12. A WORD OF PRAYER

'When you pray, do not use a lot of meaningless words, as the pagans do, who think that God will hear them because their prayers are long.'
Matthew 6:7

Many adults and children find it difficult to pray out loud. Perhaps they feel nervous or embarrassed, or they just can't think what to say. Sometimes it is helpful to start with something short, simple, and non-threatening.

Explain to your group that they only need to contribute single words to the following prayers, although they can use more! Give the group a little time to think, in advance, of some of the things that they would like to say 'thank-you', 'sorry' or 'please' to God about. Then introduce and conclude each prayer yourself, giving the group the opportunity to contribute their words at the right time. The prayers might sound something like this…

Thank you
Father God, there are so many good things that you have given us and we want to say thank-you for some of them now. Thank-you for… *friends, health, holidays, rabbits, food, water, family.*

Thank-you Lord that you have heard all our prayers.

Sorry

And now, Lord, we want to say sorry for some of the things we do that make you feel sad. Please forgive us and help us not to do these things again. We are sorry for… *laziness, fighting, lying, being unkind, bad moods.*

Thank-you, Lord, that you have heard all our prayers and that you are willing to forgive us when we are truly sorry.

Please

And finally, Lord, we want to ask you to help the following people because they need you to be especially close to them right now… *Sarah's Nan, the Prime Minister, Mr Jordan, Neeta, the curate, Tom.*

Thank-you, Lord, that you love all of these people very much and that you care about their needs.
Amen.

13. FOR PEOPLE WHO HELP US

'First of all, I ask you to pray for everyone. Ask God to help and bless them all, and tell God how thankful you are for each of them.' 1 Timothy 2:1 CEV

YOU WILL NEED: a variety of props, hats or dressing up clothes to represent different people who help us; a box or bag.

Say that we are very lucky to have different people to help us with all our everyday needs. Bring out the props one at a time and ask the group to guess what job each one represents. You might like to use some of the following:

Tube of toothpaste and toothbrush – Dentist
Toy stethoscope or box of plasters – Doctor or Nurse
Animal cage, bag of hay or sawdust – Vet
Lollipop – Lollipop man/lady
Toy fire engine or fireman's hat, smoke alarm – Fireman
Toy police car or helmet – Policeman
Letter and postcard – Postman
Spanner – Car mechanic or AA/RAC man
Exercise book and red pen – Teacher

Ask a number of children to stand in a line holding or modelling the props. Work down the line encouraging the children to say a one-line thank-you prayer, or saying a short prayer on their behalf. Thank God for the people who do each job and for the help or service that they give us. Ask God to bless the people who do those jobs and help them to help others.

TOP TIP
Why not add a few extra props to represent specific jobs held by members of your congregation?

14. UNBELIEVABLE!

'I am telling you the truth: he who believes has eternal life.' John 6:47

YOU WILL NEED: a postcard; a pair of scissors.

Show your group a postcard and tell them that you like the scene so much that you are going to get right in the middle of it. It sounds unbelievable, so ask the group to vote on whether they think that you can do it or not.

Fold the postcard in half as shown in the illustration, then make eight cuts along the folded edge of the card. Take great care to stop a good centimetre from the edge. Turn the card round and make seven similar cuts along the open side in between the first set of cuts. Open the postcard and make one last cut between the points marked A and B. Finally, open the card very gently and demonstrate how you can put your head through the middle! Give out scissors and postcards and let the group try to put their own heads through a postcard.

Remind the group that Thomas could not believe that Jesus had risen again until he saw him alive and well with his own eyes: 'Unless I see the scars of the nails in his hands and put my finger on those scars and my hand in his side, I will not believe.' (John 20:25). Ask the group how many of them believed that you could put your head in the picture on the postcard until they saw it with their own eyes. Say the following prayer together:

Lord, we have not seen you with our own eyes,
Help us to believe in you.
We have not walked through Galilee with you,
Help us to believe in you.
We have not watched you perform amazing miracles,
Help us to believe in you.
We have not seen the scars in your hands,
Help us to believe in you.
But we have read your story in the Bible,
Help us to believe in you.
We have heard others talk about knowing you,
Help us to believe in you.
And we want to love you in our hearts,
Help us to believe in you.
As a last word of encouragement, find and read John 20:29: 'Jesus said to him, "Do you believe because you see me? How happy are those who believe without seeing me!" '

15. CLOSER TO GOD

'Yet I always stay close to you, and you hold me by the hand.' Psalm 73:23

YOU WILL NEED: two sheets of A3 paper, one labelled 'Praying helps me…' and the other labelled '…to grow closer to God.'

Show the group the two sheets of paper, labelled as described above.

Then, explain that, no matter how hard you try, you simply cannot blow these two pieces of paper apart. Hold the sheets level with your cheeks and approximately 15 centimetres apart, with the edges facing the group. Blow down between the two sheets and watch as the bottom ends of the paper are drawn together.

Point out that this surprising effect reminds us that prayer breathes life into our relationship with God and draws us closer to him. Invite some of the youngsters to try out this simple experiment for themselves.

Finally, teach your group the following short prayer:

Father God,
As the weeks unfold
And the months go by,
Help me to grow closer to you.
Amen.

16. PASS THE PARCEL

'How wonderful are your gifts to me; how good they are!' Psalm 16:6

YOU WILL NEED: gift-wrap; sticky tape; individual wrapped sweets; verses printed on cards; small packet of sweets.

In advance, prepare a parcel suitable for playing pass-the-parcel. Place a small packet of sweets in the centre of the parcel, suitable for sharing among the whole group, and a Bible verse and individual sweet between each layer. Use the parcel to illustrate the fact that God has given us many good gifts to enjoy: food, water, help in times of trouble, a listening ear, his amazing love, the Holy Spirit, eternal life, his own dear Son.

Play pass the parcel. Each time the music stops and a new layer is unwrapped, read the verse that is uncovered and then stop and thank God for that amazing gift. The group might contribute short one-line prayers, for example for their favourite food. At other times, say a short prayer yourself.

You might find the following verses useful:

Food: 'The land has produced its harvest; God, our God has blessed us' Psalm 67:6.

Water: 'You show your care for the land by sending rain; you make it rich and fertile. You fill the streams with water; you provide the earth with crops' Psalm 65:9.

Help: 'God is our shelter and strength, always ready to help in times of trouble' Psalm 46:1.

A listening ear: 'I love the Lord because he hears me; he listens to my prayers. He listens to me every time I call to him' Psalm 116:1,2.

God's amazing love: 'Your constant love is better than life itself, and so I will praise you' Psalm 63:3.

The Holy Spirit: 'Peter said to them, "Each one of you must turn away from his sins and be baptised in the name of Jesus Christ, so that your sins will be forgiven; and you will receive God's gift, the Holy Spirit" ' Acts 2:38.

Jesus: 'For God loved the world so much that he gave his only Son, so that everyone who believes in him may not die but have eternal life' John 3:16.

17. PRAYER PATTERNS

'So Jesus told them, "Pray in this way:
Father, help us to honour your
name..."' Luke 11:2 CEV

YOU WILL NEED: a selection of patterns/illustrated instruction leaflets for knitting, dressmaking, Lego, origami or similar, plus the appropriate finished articles.

Bring in a selection of patterns for the group to look at, together with the relevant finished articles. Let the children examine the items and consider how closely the instructions were followed. If appropriate, you might like to help the group to follow a simple pattern to make an origami model. Alternatively, challenge the children to put together a Lego model following a set of instructions.

Explain that patterns can help us to create something special. When the disciples asked Jesus to teach them how to pray, he gave them a pattern to follow. Display the words of the Lord's prayer and read it aloud together.

Our Father in heaven,
hallowed be your name,
your kingdom come,
your will be done,
on earth as in heaven.
Give us today our daily bread.
Forgive us our sins.
as we forgive those who sin against us.
Lead us not into temptation.
but deliver us from evil.
For the kingdom, the power, and the glory are yours
now and for ever. Amen.

Jesus did not intend that we should only use these words, but simply that we should take this prayer and use it to help us compose prayers of our own. Jesus begins and ends by giving honour and glory to God. How often do we remember to give God our shopping list of 'please help' prayers but forget to praise and thank him for all that he is and all that he does?

18. PROTECT US DAY BY DAY

'Lord, have mercy on us. We have put our hope in you. Protect us day by day and save us in times of trouble.'
Isaiah 33:2

YOU WILL NEED: a selection of protective items, eg cycle helmet, sun cream, oven gloves, umbrella, shower cap, insect repellent.

Bring in a selection of items that are worn or used for protection (see list above for some ideas). Talk about each one in turn and then ask the group what all these things have in common.

God offers protection to all who love and trust him. He can protect us from unseen harm, from evil, from temptation, from the power of death, from so many different things. Find and read together Psalm 121.

Ask the group to help you list some of the times when they would most welcome God's protection. Weave all of their suggestions into a response prayer something like the following:

As we travel to and from school on busy roads,
Lord, protect us day by day.
When we're worried and lie awake at night,
Lord, protect us day by day.

When we feel uncomfortable because our friends are celebrating Hallowe'en,
Lord, protect us day by day.
When we see bullying in the playground,
Lord, protect us day by day.
When we're nervous about some new experience,
Lord, protect us day by day.

19. FOR OUR SENSE OF SMELL

'Perfume and fragrant oils make you feel happier...' Proverbs 27:9

YOU WILL NEED: mystery items to smell, eg coffee, toothpaste, soap, lemon, drinking chocolate.

Blindfold two or three volunteers and ask them to sniff and name each item. Ask them to decide whether the smell represents something edible, and then to rank the smells in order of preference. Unless your group includes very young children, you might like to include at least one unpalatable smell, such as sour milk.

Our sense of smell adds to our everyday enjoyment of the world around us. Our ability to taste different flavours is linked to our sense of smell, which is why it's difficult to enjoy a meal with a blocked-up nose. Our nose can also alert us to danger, eg when we smell burning or warn us when something might be unsafe to eat.

Ask the group to suggest some of their own favourite smells. List their ideas and weave them into a simple response prayer similar to the following:

For freshly baked bread and cookies,
We want to say... Thank-you, Lord!
For fragrant rose petals and newly cut grass,
We want to say... Thank-you, Lord!
For the citrus smell of oranges and lemons,
We want to say... Thank-you, Lord!
etc.

20. FRAGRANT PRAISE

'I am building a temple where the Lord my God will be worshipped. Sweet-smelling incense will be burnt there.' 2 Chronicles 2:4 CEV

YOU WILL NEED: a scented candle or aromatic oil.

In the Bible, incense is often used as a symbol of prayer. See Psalm 141:1,2 or Revelation 5:8 and 8:3,4. The priests burned incense twice a day on the golden altar in the temple. Perhaps the sight of the fragrant smoke rising upwards helped people to visualise their prayers rising heavenwards. Certainly the sweet fragrance would have masked all other less pleasant smells!

Burn a scented candle or use aromatic oils to add a sweet-smelling offering to your time of worship. Intersperse pauses for silent prayer with two or three quiet songs that can be sung prayerfully, eg:

'Be still and know that I am God,' *Junior Praise* 22

'Jesus, how lovely You are,' *Junior Praise* 133

21. TICKLE YOUR TASTE BUDS!

'We feast on the abundant food you provide.' Psalm 36:8

YOU WILL NEED: five different flavours of crisps, eg salt and vinegar, barbecue, smoky bacon, cheese and onion, ready salted; paper and pencils.

Explain to your group that you are going to let them taste five different flavours of crisps. Tell them in advance what the flavours are, but disguise each packet of crisps and simply identify them by numbers. Ask the group to jot down which flavour relates to each number, then check their answers at the end.

Say that God has given us a huge variety of different foods to enjoy. Invite the group to name their favourite foods and describe the flavours that they particularly like. List the adjectives that they use and weave them into a closing prayer thanking God for all the tasty flavours that he has given us to enjoy. For example:

For fruity, juicy, sweet, refreshing foods, thank-you Lord.
For cool, minty, chewy, gooey foods, thank-you Lord.
For hot and spicy, sharp and tangy foods, thank-you Lord.
For crunchy, munchy, yummy, scrummy foods, thank-you Lord.
For all the wonderful flavours that tickle our taste buds,
THANK-YOU LORD!

22. IT'S GOOD TO TALK!

'I love the Lord, because he hears me; he listens to my prayers.' Psalm 116:1

YOU WILL NEED: blackboard and chalk, or large sheet of paper and marker pen or similar, on which to write a list.

Explain to the group that you want to keep in touch with someone who has moved some distance away, and ask them to help you list some of the ways in which you could continue to communicate, for example, by letter, postcard, e-mail, telephone, mobile phone, text messaging, greetings card, fax.

In the same way it's good to keep in touch with God. He wants us to communicate with him so that we stay in touch with him, include him in our lives and draw closer to him. When we pray we give God the opportunity to work in us and through us. And the amazing thing about prayer is that we can communicate with God through our thoughts alone. We don't need pencil and paper, computers, mobile phones or any other electronic gadget. We just need to think about what we want to say to God and he hears it right away. Invite the group to join you in this two-part prayer.

A. Lord, we can tell you our joys
B. And you always listen.

A. We can say a big thank-you

B. *And you always listen.*

A. We can tell you our worries

B. *And you always listen.*

A. We can ask for help

B. *And you always listen.*

A. We can share our news

B. *And you always listen.*

A. We can say 'I'm sorry'

B. *And you always listen.*

A. Thank-you, Lord, that you always hear our prayers.

23. WASHED AND IRONED

'You are stained red with sin, but I will wash you as clean as snow.' Isaiah 1:18

YOU WILL NEED: Two similar shirts, one crumpled and dirty, the other washed and ironed and hidden inside a large, lidded laundry basket; a dish of earth.

Hold up the dirty shirt and explain to your group that our lives are a bit like this shirt. Sometimes we do wrong things; perhaps we tell a lie or take something that doesn't belong to us, perhaps we cheat in a test or smack our little brother when he annoys us. Ask the children for other suggestions of behaviour that makes God feel sad. All of these things spoil or stain our lives. Let the youngsters use some earth or similar to add one or two extra stains to the shirt to represent the effects of the wrongdoing they have just suggested!

TOP TIP
Make the stains in red felt-tip pen if you have confidence in the powers of your washing powder!

Throw the dirty shirt into the laundry basket, then pause and say a simple 'sorry' prayer incorporating the suggestions made earlier by the group. For example:

Father God, we really want to say sorry for the times when our behaviour has let you down and made you feel sad, for the times when we have got involved in fighting and bullying, for the times when we have told a lie to get out of trouble, for the times when we have used bad language...

Explain that when we say sorry to God he washes our lives clean and offers us a fresh, clean start. God not only forgives us, but he also forgets all our wrongdoing and so irons out all our 'crumples and creases'. Delve into your laundry basket and produce the identical, clean shirt. Stop and thank God for being a forgiving God, who does not remember our wrongdoing and hold it against us, but instead forgives all those who are truly sorry and gives them a second chance.

24. BE AT THE CENTRE OF MY LIFE

'Anyone who belongs to Christ is a new person.' 2 Corinthians 5:17 CEV

Lord Jesus, when I'm at home,
Be at the centre of my life.
When I'm at school,
Be at the centre of my life.
When I'm alone,
Be at the centre of my life.
When I'm with friends,
Be at the centre of my life.
When I'm working,
Be at the centre of my life.
When I'm relaxing,
Be at the centre of my life.
In everything I do,
Be at the centre of my life.
Amen.

25. KEEP US FROM TEMPTATION

'And now that Jesus has suffered and was tempted, he can help anyone else who is tempted.' Hebrews 2:18 CEV

On a scale of one to ten how easily would your group give in to temptation. Explain that '1' equals 'I'd never be tempted to do that!' and '10' equals 'I'm often tempted to do that.' Tell the group to indicate their score by raising the appropriate number of fingers. Use situations relevant to the age and interests of your group. Try these for starters.

1. You're looking at a packet of biscuits in the kitchen when you hear your mum shout from the lounge, 'And no more biscuits before dinner!' Do you take one?
2. Your friends use swear words all the time. Do you copy them to be the same or stand out as different?
3 You find a ten-pound note on the bus. Do you keep it or hand it in to the driver?

Look at Hebrews 2:18 and 4:15. Say that Jesus is always ready to help us resist temptation. Play some quiet music and suggest that the group use this time to ask God to help them deal with any difficult situations where they feel tempted to do wrong.

26. OVERCOMING THE OBSTACLES

'He guides me in the right paths, as he has promised.' Psalm 23:3

YOU WILL NEED: chairs, tables, benches, blanket, etc to make an obstacle course; blindfold.

Use whatever furniture is available to you to set up an obstacle course. Ideally, include some chairs to weave in and out of, a table to crawl under, a bench to climb over and a blanket to wriggle under.

Ask if anyone feels brave enough to tackle the obstacle course blindfolded. Give your volunteer as little help as you can safely get away with. When he has finished, point out that life is sometimes like an obstacle course. There are many ups and downs that we have to overcome. We might fall out with a friend, or fail an exam, or struggle with difficult relationships at home. Life throws all kinds of different obstacles our way, and we never know what to expect next; so it is rather like wearing a blindfold.

Fortunately, God always knows what the future holds and he wants to help us to cope during the difficult times. Illustrate this point by asking a second volunteer to put on a blindfold and tackle the obstacle course, but this time hold her hand and talk her round the course.

Explain that if we want God to help and encourage us through the difficult times then we have to pray to him. We simply need to tell him what we're going through and ask for his help. Finish with a prayer thanking God that he knows what each person is going through at the moment, and asking him to come close to any members of the group who are facing tough situations.

27. SHARING THE GOOD NEWS

'As the Scripture says, "How wonderful is the coming of messengers who bring good news!"' Romans 10:15

YOU WILL NEED: a newspaper with fictional 'good news' headlines taped inside.

Open up your newspaper and read out some of the headlines that you have prepared. Try to devise headlines that are likely to appeal to the age and interests of your group. For example:

No more school on Fridays! New four-day week to be introduced.

Five hundred free cinema tickets to see (*Insert name of latest blockbuster*).

Famous pop group (*give name*) to perform in local school assembly.

Ask the group what they would do if they read these amazing headlines in their own newspaper. Draw out that they would rush around telling everyone in the playground, ring all their friends, shout it from the rooftops and generally check that everyone else also knew the good news.

We have some far more important Good News to share: the real Good News about Jesus. Read out John 3:16. For some reason Christians are often slow to share this news. Finish with the following two-part prayer. A leader should read the lines marked A and the group reads B.

A: Lord Jesus, sometimes it's hard to share the Good News with others. When we feel shy…
B: Give us courage.
A: When we feel embarrassed…
B: Give us confidence.
A: When we lack interest…
B: Give us enthusiasm.
A: When we say 'I'll do it tomorrow.'…
B: Give us a sense of urgency.
A: And when we want to tell others about your love…
B: Give us the right words to say.

28. ODD ONE OUT

'If you greet only your friends, what's so great about that? ... But you must always act like your Father in heaven.' Matthew 5:47,48 CEV

YOU WILL NEED: sticky labels; a pen.

Think of pairs that the children will be likely to recognise: Winnie the Pooh and Christopher Robin, Wallace and Gromit, Batman and Robin. Write each name on a sticky label and put one label on the back of each child. You will also need an extra label that has no pair, eg a current pop star. The children must find out who they are and find their partner by asking simple questions that can be answered by a 'yes' or 'no'. If you have an even number in your group you will need to play the game yourself to ensure that you have an odd one out.

At the end of the game ask the child without a partner how he feels. It's miserable to be the odd one out. Jesus always included everyone. Invite the group to repeat the following words after you line by line:
Lord,
Help me to see the world through your eyes.
Help me to make other people feel welcome.
Help me to make friends with the lonely,
And to include those who feel left out. Amen.

29. WHATEVER THE COLOUR

'... there is no difference between Jews and Gentiles; God is the same Lord of all and richly blesses all who call to him.' Romans 10:12

YOU WILL NEED: a tube of Smarties; a glass of water.

Open the tube of Smarties and scatter the sweets on a plate. Ask the children in the group to tell you which colour they prefer and establish which is the favourite and least favourite colour. No doubt someone will tell you that colour doesn't matter because they all taste the same – reward their common sense with a sweet!

Point out that it's a good job that God doesn't have any favourites. He loves and values us all equally, no matter what we look like and no matter the colour of our skin. Drop four or five Smarties into a glass of water, swirl them round for a bit and you will discover that, underneath, all Smarties are the same shade of greyish white! Humans are just the same: we might all look different on the outside, but inside we're the same. Take out a world atlas and pray for Christians at home and abroad, mentioning countries that have featured in the news recently and countries where your church has a mission connection.

30. IN HAPPY TIMES AND SAD TIMES

'...you have blessed me with happiness.' Psalm 92:10

YOU WILL NEED: one large copy and several small copies of the happy/sad face shown below.

Make one large copy of the face below and show your group the happy face first. Ask the children to tell you about any special events that have made them feel happy during the past week. Make a note of all these things and say a thank-you prayer mentioning each one. Alternatively, ask different children to say a one-line thank-you prayer for each one.

Next, turn the face upside down so that the sad face appears. Ask the children if anything sad or worrying has happened this week that they would like to talk to God about. Perhaps they know someone who is ill or in hospital, someone who has lost their job or moved away. Or perhaps they have argued with a friend and would like help to make it up. Pray about all these people and situations asking for God's help in each one.

Finally, ask the children if anything they have said or done this week might have made God feel sad. Give the children a few moments to say sorry to God quietly in their hearts. Finish by thanking God that he always knows how we feel, whether we are happy or sad, and thanking him for being just as close to us in the good times as in the bad.

Give all the children a happy/sad face to take home so that they can use it during their prayer times in the coming week.

31. ROAD SIGNS

'Never stop praying, especially for others.' Ephesians 6:18 CEV

YOU WILL NEED: copies of the road signs below, enlarged on paper.

Just for a change, why not structure your prayers around the themes suggested by a set of road signs?

STOP and pray.

 Pray for the week ahead.

 Pray for the children in your church.

 Pray for the elderly.

 Pray for the twenties and thirties group (if your church has one).

 Pray for those who are at a crossroads in their lives, who are facing difficult decisions. This may include those deciding which subjects to study at school, which college or university to go to, which jobs to apply for, whether to get married or whether to move house.

 For situations where a compromise is needed.

 For people at home or abroad facing dangerous situations.

For those at work.

 For those enduring a stressful, bumpy ride.

 For the church finances!

 GO in the certain knowledge that God has heard all your prayers.

32. THANK YOU FOR LISTENING

'He listens to me every time I call to him.' Psalm 116:2

When I'm lonely and need someone to talk to,
Thank-you, Lord, for listening.
When I'm sad and need someone to lean on,
Thank-you, Lord, for listening.
When I'm worried and want to share my fears,
Thank-you, Lord, for listening.
When I'm nervous and need encouragement,
Thank-you, Lord, for listening.
When I'm confused and need help making a big decision,

Thank-you, Lord, for listening.
When I'm happy and want to share my feelings,
Thank-you, Lord, for listening.

33. THE FRUITFUL VINE

'Just as a branch cannot produce fruit unless it stays joined to the vine, you cannot produce fruit unless you stay joined to me.' John 15:4 CEV

YOU WILL NEED: a bunch of seedless grapes to share.

Pass around a bunch of grapes and let everyone try one. Comment on their sweet juiciness and talk about how they will have grown larger and juicier as they ripened on the vine. Look at how each grape is attached to a stalk that is attached to a larger one and so on until the cluster is attached to a branch on the vine. Ask the children what might have happened if the bunch of grapes had fallen off the vine in the early days of its growth. It would have stopped growing and shrivelled up and died.

Point out that our faith would wither and die if we pulled away from Jesus, but if we remain with Jesus then our lives will bear fruit and bring glory to God. Display the following prayer so that the whole group can say it together:

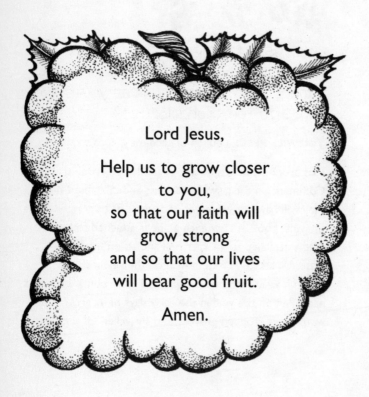

Lord Jesus,

Help us to grow closer
to you,
so that our faith will
grow strong
and so that our lives
will bear good fruit.

Amen.

34. FOR THOSE WHO SOW THE FIRST SEEDS

'...the seed is the word of God.'
Luke 8:11

YOU WILL NEED: an apple; a plate and knife.

Hold up an apple and ask the group to guess how many seeds there might be inside it. Cut the apple into slices and count the seeds to discover who guessed correctly. All of these seeds have the potential to grow into an apple tree and produce fruit of their own. In the Parable of the Sower, Luke 8:4–15, Jesus teaches that the seed is like God's Word. In the right situation it will grow and flourish. Share the slices of apple while you ask the group who first told them about Jesus, who sowed the first seed. Thank God for all these people, eg parents, other children, Sunday group helpers, church leaders and mission partners linked to your church.

35. BE STILL

'Be still, and know that I am God.'
Psalm 46:10 NIV

Sometimes it is helpful to stop and remember how amazing God is and to think about some of the things that he has done for us and given to us. Begin by reading the verse above and then ask the group to be quiet as they think about the following things and silently thank and praise God for them.

Think about a very beautiful place, somewhere outside that you know and love. Thank God for the beautiful scenery that he has created. Thank God for the world around us.

PAUSE

Think about all your friends and family, and thank God for all that they mean to you. Think about the things that you enjoy doing together and thank God for favourite activities.

PAUSE

Think about yourself and how wonderfully you have been made. Think of your five senses: seeing, hearing, touching, smelling and tasting. Praise God for all the amazing things that you can do.

PAUSE

Think about some of the times when you have done things that have made God feel sad. Say sorry to God now. Thank God that Jesus took the punishment for all our wrongdoing. Thank God that he is always willing to forgive and offer us a fresh start.

PAUSE

36. USE THE MOBILE!

'Pray that I may *be bold* in speaking about the gospel as I should.'
Ephesians 6:20

YOU WILL NEED: a mobile phone.

Is there a missionary attached to your church that you regularly pray for during your services? Why not call them on a mobile phone to hear their news and ask for their up-to-the-minute prayer requests? You will need to agree the date and exact time with them in advance to make sure that they are ready to answer the phone and will have their prayer requests ready. You will also need to hold a microphone close to the phone so that the whole group can hear their answers.

37. A SHARED BLESSING

'I pray that our Lord Jesus Christ will be kind to you and will bless your life!' Philippians 4:23 CEV

YOU WILL NEED: Bibles.

Help the group to find 2 Peter 3:18 in their Bibles, or read a large copy of the words aloud together. Then, ask each person to say the words as a prayer for the person on their left, eg 'Sally, I pray that you will continue to grow in the grace and knowledge of our Lord and Saviour Jesus Christ.' If some group members are likely to find it difficult to pray aloud for each other, say the prayer yourself, inserting the relevant names at the beginning. Explain to the group that it is often helpful to pray using God's Word for one another, since many Bible verses are powerful and yet also personal.

Many of the blessings that Paul writes at the end of his letters can be personalised in the same way, simply by including the names of your group at the end. 'I pray that our Lord Jesus Christ will be kind to you and bless your life, Samuel' (Philippians 4:23 CEV) or 'I pray, Charlotte, that you will understand "how broad and long, how high and deep, is Christ's love"' (Ephesians 3:18 GNB).

38. GROWING CLOSER TO GOD

'But continue to grow in the grace and knowledge of our Lord and Saviour Jesus Christ.' 2 Peter 3:18

Invite the group to join in with the words *'help us to grow closer to you'* each time they hear the cue words, 'Father God'.

Like a tree that grows tall and stately,
Father God... *Help us to grow closer to you.*
Like a field of crops growing thick and golden,
Father God... *Help us to grow closer to you.*
Like a flower growing towards the sun,
Father God... *Help us to grow closer to you.*
Like fruit growing ripe and rosy,
Father God... *Help us to grow closer to you.*

TOP TIP

Give children a bean to take home and plant in an empty jam jar, on wet kitchen towel. Just as the bean grows, they can remember that they are growing with God.

39. A PRAYER FOR PEACE

'Happy are those who work for peace;
God will call them his children.'
Matthew 5:9

YOU WILL NEED: recent newspapers. (NB Check – you
may want to remove any unsuitable pages.)

Talk about some of the key newspaper headlines and
photos relating to situations where God's peace is
needed. After a short discussion, invite the group to join
you in the following response prayer:

To a world of violence and greed,
Help us to bring your peace.
To a world of anger and hatred,
Help us to bring your peace.
To a world where countries war with others,
Help us to bring your peace.
To a world where people have forgotten how to care
and share,
Help us to bring your peace.
To a world where children suffer in war-torn countries,
Help us to bring your peace.
To a world where people prefer to get even, rather
than forgive,
Help us to bring your peace.

40. FOR THE WEEK AHEAD...

'May the grace of the Lord Jesus Christ be with you all.' Philippians 4:23

Use the following words as a closing prayer with your group. Display the words for everyone to see and as you say each line use an appropriate mime action to convey the meaning. Those who can read can join in with the words, and even the youngest children can join in with the actions.

This week I pray that...

God's hand will lead you,
God's eyes will watch over you,
God's ears will hear your prayers,
God's arms will protect you,
God's Word will encourage you,
And God's love will fill your heart.

41. FAREWELL PRAYER

'Jesus himself drew near and walked along with them...' Luke 24:15

You might like to try saying this prayer standing close together, with all the children putting their arms around the shoulders of the child next to them, almost in the style of a rugby huddle. The whole group could then shout the final 'Amen' as they release arms and go out with God.

As we leave this place,
Go with us, Lord.
As we begin a new week,
Go with us, Lord.
As we encounter
new experiences,
Go with us, Lord.
As we meet old
friends and new,
Go with us, Lord.
In everything we do
in the week ahead,
Go with us, Lord.
Amen.

PRAYERS TO WRITE, DRAW AND MAKE

We can communicate with God in many different ways, not just by the spoken word. We can write, draw and make our prayers in new ways that will really stimulate us to stop and think about what we want to say to God. A prayer collage or praise poster can be an attractive and lasting reminder of God's goodness; a model can prompt us to pray, and a written prayer can be re-read and prayed, over and over again.

Don't be afraid to make a prayer collage or similar with a mixed age group or in an all-age service. Adults can learn and benefit from the youngsters' joyful, uninhibited enthusiasm. Let everyone write or draw their prayers and then the children can collect in the finished results and stick them down while the adults sing some appropriate worship songs. Whenever possible, invite the group to write or draw their prayers on large sticky labels, so that you

don't even need to worry about getting glue on the carpet! Once the collage is finished hold it up for the whole congregation to see and then offer it to God as a token of love and praise.

42. PRAYER PYRAMIDS

'First of all, then, I urge that petitions, prayers, requests and thanksgivings be offered to God for all people...
I Timothy 2:I

YOU WILL NEED: enlarged copies of the pyramid shape (illustrated); scissors; crayons; glue.

Give everyone a copy of the unmade pyramid to colour in the lettering and then cut out the shape following the bold outside edge lines. Turn the pyramid over so that the words are on the reverse, and then fold inwards along each dotted line. Put glue on the top of each tab, then fold the three outside triangles upwards until they meet, and press each tab under the adjoining triangle to complete the pyramid.

Ask the children to hold their pyramid in their hands with the word 'Praise' facing them. Encourage the group to call out one-line prayers suited to that word. Continue in the same way until all four faces have been used.

If the group are not used to praying out loud, say a very simple prayer for each word, so that the children will know how to use the pyramid in the privacy of their own rooms at home. Encourage the group to take their pyramids home as prayer reminders.

43. RECIPE FOR PRAYER

'For we do not know how we ought to pray...' Romans 8:26

YOU WILL NEED: a mixing bowl; a spoon; slips of paper with short prayers; spare slips of paper; pens; containers and packets as follows:

A clean margarine tub labelled PRAISE, containing slips of paper with short expressions of praise, eg 'God is great!'

An empty flour packet labelled SORRY, containing short prayers for forgiveness, eg 'Sorry for fighting with my brother.'

An empty sugar packet labelled THANK-YOU, with one-line thank-you prayers, eg 'thank-you for loving me.'

A plastic egg box labelled PLEASE with brief prayer requests, eg 'Please help my Grandpa to get better soon.'

Explain that a cake needs the right combination of ingredients in order to cook and to rise, and in the same way our prayers need to include a variety of ingredients. Explain that you are now going to 'mix up' a prayer using some of these ingredients. Produce the food containers in turn, showing the labels. Tip the prayers into the mixing bowl. Each time invite one or two children to read out some of the examples and allow children to write their own prayers on the blank slips of paper.

Point out that if we only say 'sorry' prayers we are missing out on thanking God for the good things that he gives us or asking him to help with some of the difficult situations that we encounter. If we only pray 'please help' prayers, it is like giving God a shopping list and ignoring the great things that he does for us. To build a relationship with God we need to talk to him about everything, remembering to thank him, praise him, say sorry to him, and ask for his help for ourselves and for other people.

Ask each child to choose and read out a slip of paper as a concluding prayer.

44. THREE GRACES

'He sat down to eat with them, took the bread and said the blessing...'
Luke 24:30

YOU WILL NEED: paper plates; split pins; glue; pictures of food from magazines, etc; pens.

Divide one paper plate into thirds with a line separating each section. Help the children to write three simple short graces, one in each section, for breakfast, lunch and supper. With very young children print three simple sentences for them to cut out and stick down, eg 'Thank-you for my breakfast, Lord!', 'Thank-you, Jesus, for our lovely lunch.' and 'Thank-you, Lord, for our supper'.

Then take the second plate and cut one triangular slice out of it, the same size as a section on the first plate. Leave a small circle of card in the middle so that you can insert a split pin. Cut out pictures from supermarket and cookery magazines to decorate this plate. Then, using the split pin, attach it to the first plate so that it can be turned around like a dial to reveal the appropriate grace for each mealtime.

45. SERVIETTE RINGS

'Then he took the five loaves and the two fish, looked up to heaven, and gave thanks to God.' Matthew 14:19

YOU WILL NEED: copies of the outline opposite; scissors; crayons; paper serviettes.

God provides us with so many good things, not least the food that we eat every day. Talk to your group about the importance of saying thank-you to God for the food that we enjoy, then help them to make these simple serviette rings as a take-home reminder to pray before meals.

Photocopy and enlarge the illustrated outline onto thin card. Cut along the bold lines, not forgetting to cut out the two slots. Encourage the children to colour in the lettering and the pattern on the butterfly. Curve the card around and then slot one side into the other to make the serviette ring.

You could also provide the youngsters with a paper serviette to slot through the ring. If you have a church meal planned, for example, harvest supper, why not make a serviette ring for everyone?

46. PRAYER SHAPES

'The Lord is great and deserves our greatest praise!' Psalm 96:4 CEV

YOU WILL NEED: paper, pen and scissors or computer and printer.

Write a prayer that makes a shape on the page. A prayer about homes and families in a house shape; a prayer about Easter in an egg shape; a Christmas prayer in a Christmas tree shape.

★
The
Christmas
tree is decorated with
tinsel
and baubles. The
cards
are on the mantelpiece and the
presents are under the
tree.
Lord, sometimes we are so busy enjoying the
parties, the decorations,
the food and the fun, that we forget to include you in our
Christmas celebrations.
We're
sorry for the times when we forget that it's your birthday that
we're
celebrating. Help us
to remember that you came to earth
to show us
just
how much you love us. Help us to celebrate the real meaning
of Christmas; and help us to remember that the tinsel
and baubles are just
extras.
In
Your name, Jesus,
Amen.

47. SHARING

'Whoever shares with others should do it generously...' Romans 12:8

YOU WILL NEED: plasticene or clay.

This prayer works particularly well after a story in which some kind of sharing has taken place. For example, in the parable of the good Samaritan, the Samaritan shares his oil, wine, donkey and money with an injured traveller. And the story of Jesus miraculously feeding the 5000 starts when a little boy is willing to share his lunch.

God is always pleased when we are willing to share with others. Give each child a lump of plasticene or clay and ask them to make a model of something that they are willing to share during the coming week. For example: toys, games, books, pocket money, a break time snack.

When everyone has finished, spend a few moments chatting about their creations and then close with a prayer offering each model to God and asking him to help each group member to be ready and willing to share in the coming week.

48. PUT JESUS IN THE CENTRE

'Keep your roots deep in him, build your lives on him...' Colossians 2:7

YOU WILL NEED: a length of old wallpaper; thick wax crayons.

Ask a child to lie down on the back of the length of wallpaper while you draw round him. When he stands up you should have a reasonable outline of a child. Draw a circle in the middle of the shape and leave it blank, but tell the group that they can write or draw anywhere else on the figure. Ask them to write or draw in the figure all the things that make up their lives and the things they do, eg school, church, swimming club and the things they enjoy, such as football, TV, chocolate, pop music, seeing friends.

Explain that Jesus wants to be a part of our lives; in fact, he wants to be right at the centre of our lives! Write 'JESUS' in the middle of the circle. Finish with a prayer thanking Jesus for all the things written or drawn on the figure, naming them one by one, and asking him to be a part of everything we do.

49. WORRY BOX

'Leave all your worries with him, because he cares for you.' 1 Peter 5:7

YOU WILL NEED: a gift-wrapped box with a hole in the top, labelled 'Worry box'; slips of paper; pens.

Mary and Joseph were worried when they lost Jesus on the way home from Jerusalem (Luke 2:41–52). Martha was worried about the housework and cooking when Jesus and his disciples came to visit (Luke 10:38–42). Our young people have many worries of their own, but we can reassure them that Jesus invites us to take all our worries to him.

Give out slips of paper and invite the youngsters to write down anything that is worrying them, eg 'Lord, I'm worried about which secondary school I'm going to go to', 'Lord Jesus, I get really worried at playtime because some of the older children are real bullies', 'Father God, I'm worried about my Gran who is not well'.

During a time of quiet prayer, invite the children to post their worries in the box and, in this way, actively give them to Jesus. The leader can then lift the box up high, offering it to Jesus, and conclude with a prayer thanking Jesus that he is willing to shoulder all our worries and asking him to bring his peace, love and healing into all those worrying situations.

50. LEAF RUBBINGS

'He controls the times and the seasons...' Daniel 2:21

YOU WILL NEED: paper; green wax crayons; small branch; vase; sticky tape.

Bring in some dry leaves and give your group paper and green wax crayons so that they can make leaf rubbings. Cut out the leaf shapes so that each child has at least one leaf. Let the children use the back of the leaf rubbing to write a prayer thanking God for all the new spring growth, the new leaves on the trees, the daffodils, tulips and crocus bulbs. Put a small branch into a vase and then tape these prayer leaves all over the branch to produce a green leafy prayer plant.

51. ON THE MAP

'But the Holy Spirit will come upon you and give you power. Then you will tell everyone about me in Jerusalem, in all Judea, in Samaria and everywhere in the world.' Acts 1:8 CEV

YOU WILL NEED: local and regional maps; world map or atlas; pens; *Post-it* notes or squares of paper.

Just before Jesus went back to heaven he told his disciples to take his message to all people everywhere. Find and read Acts chapter 1, verse 8. Show the children a map of your town, your county and neighbouring counties. Explain that in our terms Jerusalem might be our town, Judea our county or province and Samaria the county next door. Next, look at a world map and notice other countries that border yours or are close by. Jesus wants his message of good news to be taken to all these countries too.

Give out pens and squares of paper or *Post-it* notes. Invite the children to write a short prayer, either asking Jesus to help them spread the good news, or asking him to help people connected with your church who are engaged in outreach work either at home or abroad. Stick each prayer onto the relevant place on the map. Ask God to give us opportunities and the right words to tell others about his Son, Jesus.

52. DOOR HANGERS

'May the Lord show his constant love during the day...' Psalm 42:8

'I lie down and sleep, and all night long the Lord protects me.' Psalm 3:5

YOU WILL NEED: enlarged copies of the outline below; crayons; scissors; glue.

Copy and enlarge the shape below to make individual door hangers. Help the children to fill in their names and colour in the pictures, then fold along the dotted line and glue the two sides together. Encourage the children to say the short prayers as they go to bed at night and as they go out in the morning.

'S

Room

Father God, please watch over me while I sleep.

Father God, wherever I go and whatever I do today, please be with me.

53. JESUS CARES ABOUT US WHEN WE'RE ILL

'He heals the broken-hearted and bandages their wounds.' Psalm 147:3

YOU WILL NEED: a large picture of a bed; a marker pen; plasters; a pen.

Draw a large outline of a bed, and ask the group to tell you the names of any people they know who are ill or in hospital. Write these names on the bed covers. Pray for all the people mentioned, asking that Jesus will be close to them and their families during their illnesses, and thanking him for the skills of the doctors and nurses looking after them. Explain to the group that Jesus always cares about us when we are ill. Write the words 'Jesus cares' on strips of Elastoplast and ask different children to stick one beside each name.

54. HELIUM HALLELUJAHS

'Praise the Lord's glorious name...'
Psalm 29:2

YOU WILL NEED: helium-filled balloons; lengths of ribbon; marker pens.

For a special festival or a church anniversary, you might like to consider decorating the church with helium-filled balloons. A couple of balloons tied at the end of each row will make the church look really festive. When you reach your prayer time distribute marker pens and invite the congregation to write one-line prayers on their balloons praising God for all that he is and thanking him for all that he has done. Ask some of the youngsters to bring the balloons to the front and read out the prayers. At the end of the service, the balloons can be given to the children to take home, or given to members of the congregation who are ill and in need of cheering up!

During an outreach service you could even take the balloons outside and release them into the community.

55. BOUNCE THE BALL

'...walking and jumping and praising God.' Acts 3:8 CEV

YOU WILL NEED: a football or large ball; sticky labels; pens.

Ask the children to think about the sports and games that they most enjoy. Talk about the benefits of playing sport; for example, health, strength, fitness, relaxation and teamwork. Give out sticky labels and invite group members to choose a sport or activity for which they would like to thank God. Help the children to write the name of their favourite sport on their labels. Younger children who find it difficult to write could draw a small picture instead. Let the children cover the ball in sticky labels. Then, sit in a large circle and roll the ball across the group. The children will take it in turns to stop the ball, say a one-line thank-you prayer based on one of the labels, and then roll the ball to someone else. If you have a large space, or can meet outside, you might like to try bouncing the ball across the group instead.

56. NEW LIFE

'You refresh the earth like morning dew; you give life to the dead.'
Isaiah 26:19 CEV

YOU WILL NEED: a few dry autumn leaves; moisturising cream or baby lotion.

Show the group a dry autumn leaf. Comment on the fact that it is dried up, fragile and easily broken. Scrunch the leaf up in your hand to show how it breaks. Let one or two group members do the same.

Sometimes Christians feel fragile. We have bad days when everything seems to go wrong or when our world seems to be falling apart. There are days when our faith feels fragile. God wants to revive us and refresh us. He wants to fill us with his Holy Spirit.

Pour a little moisturiser into the middle of one of the leaves, and very gently rub it into the leaf, working it out towards the outside edges. You will want to try this out beforehand, but with a little patience you should find that the leaf becomes supple again. Say that God's Holy Spirit can revive us in just the same way that the moisturiser has revived the leaf. Pray, asking God to fill each person with his soothing, refreshing, restoring, reviving Spirit.

57. BLESS OUR HOMES AND FAMILIES

'Go back home to your family and tell them how much the Lord has done for you and how kind he has been to you.' Mark 5:19

YOU WILL NEED: paper house shapes; pens or crayons.

Give each member of the group a simple paper house shape. Ask them to draw a stick figure on their houses to represent each member of their family or each person who shares the same roof. Ask the group to hold their house in their hands and to spend a few moments thinking about each person that they have drawn. Encourage the group to consider the good qualities of each person and to thank God for them. Then, if appropriate, ask the group to consider any aspects of each relationship that cause problems. Say that it's not easy to get along well with each member of the family all the time. Allow a few moments of quiet for everyone to ask God to make a difference in their home and ask him to help them cope with any difficult relationships.

58. PATCHWORK OFFERING

'Tabitha ... was always doing good things for people and had given much to the poor.' Acts 9:36

YOU WILL NEED: coloured paper hexagon shapes; pens; backing paper; glue.

Tabitha, or Dorcas as she was also known, pleased God by using her time and talents for others. She was good at sewing, and helped widows and their children by making coats and clothes for them. How could your group copy Tabitha and use their skills to help others?

Give out hexagons and encourage the group to write their ideas on them. For example: I can give my mum a break and read a bedtime story to my little sister. I can make cards to cheer up people who are ill.

Anyone who can't think what to put could write a simple prayer, eg 'Father God, show me what I can do to help others'. Young children could draw a picture of themselves helping someone.

Stick all the hexagons onto a sheet of backing paper to make a patchwork quilt! Write the words 'Father God, we offer you our talents. Please show us how we can use them to help others.' across the centre of the 'quilt'. Offer the finished collage to God with a prayer.

59. PRAYER E-MAILS

'I pray to you, O God, because you answer me...' Psalm 17:6

YOU WILL NEED: sheets of A5 paper cut into 'E' shapes; length of string/washing line; clothes pegs.

In this technological age, why not send God some prayer 'e-mails'? Invite the group to write short prayers on their E-shaped pieces of paper. These can then be pegged onto a washing line so that the prayers really do go on-line! A leader can then retrieve the prayers and forward them to the group by reading them aloud during a quiet time of prayer. In subsequent weeks the prayers can be reviewed. Answered prayers can be turned over and a short thank-you prayer can be written on the back; and ongoing prayers can be repeated.

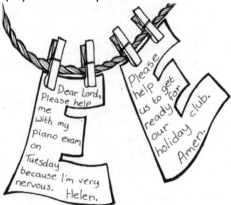

(With thanks to Andrew Ostler.)

60. SPEECH BUBBLES

'Praise God with shouts of joy, all
people!' Psalm 66:1

YOU WILL NEED: pieces of paper cut into the shape of
speech bubbles; pens.

Ask the group to imagine that they are in the crowd
following Jesus. Perhaps they have just witnessed a
miracle, enjoyed an exciting story or watched Jesus ride
into Jerusalem. This joyful prayer can be used after any
Bible story where a crowd might have been present.

Give out the paper speech bubbles and ask the group to
write on them what they might have said or shouted if
they had been there. Young children could draw happy
smiley faces. Explain that crowds all speak at the same
time, so you are going to ask everyone to shout out their
words of praise
and then read out
the comments on
those nearby, all at
the same time.
God will delight in
hearing shouts of
praise from a
joyful crowd.

TOP TIP

On Palm Sunday, get children
to write their words of praise
onto simple paper palm leaf
shapes and make a huge palm
tree.

61. PERSISTENT PRAYER

'Never give up praying.'
Colossians 4:2 CEV

YOU WILL NEED: materials to make badges or bracelets, as explained below.

Have you seen the tie-on fabric bracelets for sale in many Christian bookshops? They bear a number of letters that remind the wearer of something special. For example: W.W.J.D.? means What Would Jesus Do?

Why not help those in your group to make a P.U.S.H. (Pray Until Something Happens) badge or bracelet? With younger children, use ready-made badge backs and felt pens to make badges, or strips of decorated card to make bracelets. Older children could cross-stitch the letters P.U.S.H. onto a length of silk or velvet ribbon. Alternatively, thread alphabet beads onto leather or cord. Use this prayer at the end.

Lord God, when the going gets tough,
Help us to keep on praying.
When we're happy, thankful, sad or worried,
Help us to keep on praying.
When we've done something wrong,
Help us to keep on praying.
When we see others in need,
Help us to keep on praying.
Night and day, rain or shine,
Help us to keep on praying.

62 FISHING FOR MEN

'Jesus said to them, "Come with me! I will teach you how to bring in people instead of fish."' Matthew 4:19 CEV

YOU WILL NEED: a sheet of A4 paper, pen and scissors for each group member.

Explain that Jesus chose several fishermen to join his band of disciples. He told them that from then on they would no longer be catching fish; instead they would be catching men and women for the Kingdom of God.

Help the group to fold their paper into four sections, concertina-style, along the length of the paper. Draw a simple outline of a fish on the top fold. Make sure that the edges of the fins and tail reach the sides. Help the children to cut round their outlines so that, when the paper is unfolded, they have four fish all joined together.

They can draw an eye and mouth on each fish, and write the name of a friend or relative who they would like to introduce to Jesus.

Pray that God will help the people named on the fish to hear about his special love for them. And pray that God will help each child to find the right opportunity and words to tell someone else the good news. Encourage the youngsters to take their fish home to help them remember to pray for these four people during the week.

63. HELPING HANDS

'Do not forget to do good and to help one another, because these are the sacrifices that please God.'
Hebrews 13:16

YOU WILL NEED: a piece of A5 paper per group member; pen and scissors.

God wants us to be willing to help others whenever we can. Some people are very good at seeing when and how they can offer help, but sometimes others are too wrapped up in their own concerns to realise that other people might value their help.

Ask the group to place their hand on their piece of paper and draw round it. They should then cut out the hand shape and write a very short prayer on it, for example, 'Lord Jesus, please help me to see how I can help others this week.' In an all-age service use pre-cut hand shapes.

Explain to the group that just as we offer money to God, so we can also offer our time and help. While the group sings a quiet worship song, pass round an offering bag or plate and invite the group to place their hand shapes in it. Conclude with a prayer asking God to help each person find some special way to help a friend, colleague, relative or neighbour this week.

64. PRAYING FOR OTHERS

'... pray for everyone. Ask God to help and bless them all, and tell God how thankful you are for each of them.'
I Timothy 2:I CEV

YOU WILL NEED: a large sheet of paper on which you have drawn six circles; coloured marker pens.

Help the group to find and read I Timothy 2:I. Explain that the Bible tells us that we should pray for others. Sometimes we want to ask God to help other people, or to be especially close to them and bless them. At other times we might want to thank God for people and for all the things that they do for us. Show your sheet of paper. Ask the group whether they would like to pray for anyone special and, as they tell you about people, draw eyes, nose, mouth and hair on one of the circles and write a name underneath. Encourage the children to think not only about friends and family, but also about needy people in the news.

TOP TIP
Older children will be able to draw features, but for under-fives it might be better to draw the face yourself.

Either weave all of the people and their needs into one concluding prayer, or ask different children to pray for each person.

65. FOR THOSE IN AUTHORITY

'Pray for kings and others in power,
so that we may live quiet and peaceful
lives as we worship and honour God.'
1 Timothy 2:2 CEV

YOU WILL NEED: a collection of newspaper pictures of
people in positions of authority, mounted on card or
photocopied onto acetate.

Build up a collection of newspaper pictures of people in
authority, such as the Queen, key politicians, world leaders
etc. For children it's always a good idea to put a face to
each name, so that they have a better idea of who they are
praying for. Use a selection of pictures from your
collection whenever you want to pray for people in power.

Pray that God will guide all these people so that they rule
with justice and compassion and pass laws that are for
the good of the people and pleasing to God. If
appropriate, include other prayers relevant to current
affairs. Display newspaper photos and captions where
suitable.

One group of SALT users who prayed for the Prime
Minister and the Queen decided to write to both and let
them know. They were thrilled to receive encouraging
replies from 10 Downing Street and Buckingham Palace!

66. YOU CAN'T JUDGE A BOOK BY ITS COVER

'You have looked deep into my heart,
Lord, and you know all about me.'
Psalm 139:1 CEV

YOU WILL NEED: a comic and a Sunday supplement with
the outer covers swapped over, and two books of similar
size with the dust jackets swapped over; heart-shaped
pieces of paper; pens.

Ask a couple of members of your group to choose one
of the magazines or books to take away and read. Ask
them to explain why they chose the one they did. Was it
because of the cover, the colour of the jacket, the author,
the title or something else? Wait for your two volunteers
to discover how they have been fooled.

Explain that we tend to make sweeping judgements based
on the outward appearance of people and things. God is
not fooled by our outward appearance: he alone looks
deeper and sees our hearts, thoughts and feelings. Give
out paper hearts and invite the group to write their own
short prayers acknowledging that what we look like on
the inside is far more important than our outward
appearance, and praying that our thoughts and feelings
will always be acceptable and pleasing to God.

67. WIPE AWAY MY SINS

'You are kind, God! ... You are always merciful! Please wipe away my sins.'
Psalm 51:1 CEV

YOU WILL NEED: blackboard and chalk (or whiteboard and markers, or OHP); acetate and non-permanent pens; kitchen towel; pen.

In advance, write 'I'm sorry. Please wipe away my sins.' in large letters on six or eight sheets of kitchen towel (once on each sheet) and then roll it up again.

Together, make a list of some of the things we do that make God feel sad, such as fighting, not being helpful, stealing, being greedy. Write their suggestions on an OHP acetate or blackboard. Explain that God wants to forgive us for all these wrong things and give us the opportunity to make a fresh clean start. All we have to do is say sorry to God, really meaning it, and then he will forgive us. Find and read Psalm 51:1 together and then say a simple prayer saying sorry to God for all the things on your list. Show the group your kitchen towel, tear off a sheet and invite a child to rub out one of the words with it. Do the same until the whole list has been wiped away. Remind the children that when we say sorry to God he not only forgives us, but he also forgets and wipes the slate clean.

68. WALKING GOD'S WAY

'Happy are those who follow his commands, who obey him with all their heart. They never do wrong; they walk in the Lord's ways.' Psalm 119:2,3

YOU WILL NEED: a shallow dish of paint; a pair of child's wellington boots; a large sheet of paper or the back of a length of wallpaper.

Ask your group what they think it means to 'walk God's way'. Explain that when we live our lives in a way that pleases God, when we follow his commands and include him in our life, then we are walking God's way.

Write the words 'Dear Lord, help us to walk your way' in the middle of your sheet of paper. Then invite all those children who want to follow God to dip the wellington boot into the dish of paint and make a series of footprints around the edge of the paper. Encourage them to sign their name under their footprint. The advantage of using wellies is that the paint is kept away from fingers and the boots can easily be washed at the end! Of course, if you have plenty of time and hot soapy water, let the children dip their bare feet into a shallow tray of paint and then walk over the wallpaper.

Conclude with a prayer offering the finished painting to God as a sign of the group's desire to walk his way.

69. ARROW PRAYERS

'But you answered my prayer when I shouted for help.' Psalm 31:22

YOU WILL NEED: cardboard arrow-shapes; pens.

Sometimes when we are in a difficult situation, feeling frightened or nervous, there's no time to kneel and pray or to wait for a quiet time at the end of the day; you simply have to shoot an arrow prayer up to heaven right away. Try to give your group one or two examples of when they might want to pray instant, on-the-spot prayers. For example: when you're facing a fierce dog, when you're nervous about reading something out in assembly. Help them to see that a hasty 'Lord, please help me now!' is just the right prayer for that occasion. Give all the children a cardboard arrow shape and encourage them to write the words of Psalm 31:22 along the shaft as a take-home reminder that God hears even the shortest prayers.

70. OVERWHELMING LOVE

'Love never gives up...' 1 Corinthians 13:7

YOU WILL NEED: red paper hearts; glue; backing paper; pens; green crayons.

Tell your group a story about something naughty that you did when you were younger, emphasising that, even though your mum or dad was cross and upset, she/he still went on loving you.

Explain that it's just the same with God. We often do things that make him feel sad, but he goes on and on loving us. Give out heart-shaped pieces of red paper and invite everyone to write a short prayer on their piece of paper thanking God that he never stops loving us, even when we're naughty, and asking that he will help us to do the things that please him. Young children might simply like to draw kisses on their heart.

Stick the heart shapes together in clusters to look like flowers. Add stalks and a few green leaves in green crayon for extra effect. During an all-age service, you could invite youngsters to make up the collage while the adults sing one or two songs. Finish with a prayer offering the whole bunch of flowers to God.

71. PRAISE 'COPTERS

'Praise the Lord, because he is good.'
Psalm 135:3

YOU WILL NEED: one paper helicopter (see illustration) and paper clip per person; pens.

In advance, enlarge, photocopy and cut out one

helicopter for each member of your group. Encourage the children to decorate it. Then ask them to turn their helicopter over and write a one-line praise prayer on the reverse. Young children could draw something that they'd like to thank God for.

Place a paper clip on the nose of each helicopter and fold one tail piece forward and the other back. When the helicopter is dropped from a height it will whirl round until it reaches the ground. Encourage the entire group to drop their helicopters and then pick up someone else's and read their prayer. Continue until everyone has read six or seven prayers. Finish by asking everyone to say his or her own praise prayer.

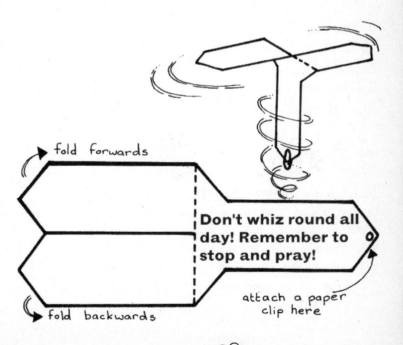

fold forwards

Don't whiz round all day! Remember to stop and pray!

attach a paper clip here

fold backwards

72. WELCOME INTO MY LIFE

'When that day comes, you will know that I am in my Father and that you are in me, just as I am in you.'
John 14:20

YOU WILL NEED: backing paper; glue; gift-wrap; marker pen; one cut-out paper person per child.

Explain to your group that you are going to make a poster that says, 'JESUS you are WELCOME in my life.' Cut the letters for JESUS and WELCOME from gift-wrap and stick them to the backing paper. Add the remaining words with a marker pen.

Give out the paper people shapes – a simple gingerbread man shape will be fine – and encourage all the children to draw their features and write their own name on the outline.

Play some quiet music and invite the children to come out and stick their figure on the poster. They might want to do this to show that they want to welcome Jesus for the first time, to thank him for being a part of their life already or to say that they want to know more about him. Make it clear that it's also acceptable to take the figure home, if they prefer. Leave the music playing for a minute longer and suggest that the children use the time to quietly talk to God.

73. THANK YOU FOR ANIMALS

'Then God commanded, "Let the earth produce all kinds of animal life: domestic and wild, large and small" – and it was done.' Genesis 1:24,25

YOU WILL NEED: circles of different-coloured paper; crayons; glue; backing paper.

Invite the group to tell you about their favourite animals and pets. Talk about the enjoyment that animals bring. It's lovely to cuddle a cat, play with a hamster, or ride a pony. Give out circles of paper and ask the children to write or draw a prayer thanking God for their favourite animal.

Glue all the circles onto the backing paper in a long wiggly line and add a smiley face at the front, antennae and feet. If you have a large group, you will be able to make several!

74. SPECIAL TO GOD

'You are the one who put me together inside my mother's body, and I praise you because of the wonderful way you created me.' Psalm 139:13,14 CEV

YOU WILL NEED: an ink stamp; white paper; black pens.

As a group, look at Psalm 139 and talk about the fact that God created us. He made each one of us to be completely unique, and he loves us just the way we are.

Help the children to make fingerprints using an ink stamp. Give each child a piece of white paper and show them how they can make three prints, one above the other, and then use a black pen to add, legs, arms, hair and a face. The end result is a unique fingerprint person. Compare prints to discover that all the patterns are different, just as we are all different, though we are all equally and completely loved by God.

Encourage older children to write a one-line thank-you prayer beneath their person, eg 'Thank-you, Lord, that you created me and love me'.

TOP TIP
Make the top print last so that it will be pale enough to draw a face on top.

75. PRAYER BOOKLETS

'Always be joyful and never stop praying.' 1 Thessalonians 5:16,17 CEV

YOU WILL NEED: a selection of pre-cut magazine pictures; A3 paper; scissors; glue.

Follow the instructions below to make simple paper booklets. Then, using a selection of pictures from magazines and catalogues, help the children to make a thank-you booklet by sticking an appropriate picture on each page to thank God for food, drink, friends, animals, clothes, their homes, etc. Write the words 'Thank-you God, for…' on the front cover and write appropriate captions inside. Older children will be able to draw some of the pictures themselves, while younger children will enjoy sticking down pre-cut pictures.

1 Take a piece of A4 paper, and fold the length in half from right to left.

2 Fold it in half from top to bottom and then unfold it again.

3 Fold it in half from right to left and then unfold it again.

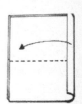

4 You should have fold lines in the shape of a cross. Cut along the right hand crease from the folded side into the middle.

5 Open out the paper.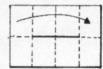

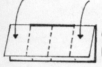

6 Fold the length in half from top to bottom.

7 Hold the paper as shown and push the two sides together, so that the middle section folds outwards.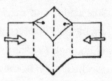

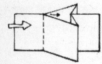

8 Push the two sides together to make the middle pages of the book.

9 You now have a simple booklet. Write a title on the front cover and draw or stick appropriate pictures on the seven remaining sides.

76. YOU'RE IN OUR THOUGHTS AND PRAYERS

'Never stop praying, especially for others.' Ephesians 6:18 CEV

YOU WILL NEED: thin card; scissors; felt-tip pens; envelopes.

People always feel encouraged when they know that friends are praying for them. If someone in your group is unwell, has moved house, is starting a new school or job why not make them one of these stand-up cards? Make a point of praying for that person during your group time and then ask someone who lives nearby to pop the card through his or her letterbox. Why not make several extra cards to keep in reserve for when you need them?

77. REMEMBER TO PRAY

 6-11

'I thank him as I remember you always in my prayers night and day.'
2 Timothy 1:3

YOU WILL NEED: clothes pegs; PVA glue; card; sticky shapes; sticky-back plastic.

Cut some small pieces of card (approx. 8cm × 4cm) and help the children to write the words 'REMEMBER: When you have a busy day, take the time to stop and pray!' on them. Alternatively, print the words on a word processor and let the youngsters stick them on their cards. Decorate the cards with stars and sticky shapes and cover the front with sticky-backed plastic. Stick these cards onto a clothes peg with PVA glue to make a reminder peg.

The pegs can be used to hold prayer letters, news clippings, church newsheets or prayer lists. Why not make an extra peg for the group, where the children can clip their own prayer suggestions and requests? Make a point of including all the prayers during your worship time. In subsequent weeks you can remove old requests, thank God for answered prayers and repeat prayers for ongoing situations.

78. THANK YOU FOR BEING OUR SPECIAL FRIEND

'I speak to you as my friends, and I have told you everything that my Father has told me.' John 15:15 CEV

YOU WILL NEED: cardboard gingerbread men shapes; the outline of a train; brown envelopes; crayons; backing paper; glue.

Cut out the outline of a large train and mount it on backing paper with several carriages made out of brown envelopes coupled on behind (see illustration). Then give the children simple cut-out figures on which to draw a face, hair and clothes to make the figure look like them. Explain that Jesus wants to be our special friend. We can't see him, but we can talk to him in our prayers and we know that he hears us and is always there for us. Take time with each child to discuss what they would like to write in the centre of their figure, for example, 'Thank-you, Jesus, for being my special friend' or 'Thank-you that you love me and care about me'. Pop the figures into the empty train carriages and write underneath, 'We're all friends of Jesus!' This prayer collage could be used on a weekly basis. Why not take all the figures out at the end of the session and pray for each child as you replace them? For example, 'Lord Jesus, thank-you that you are Sarah's special friend. Please be with her in this coming week.'

79. FLAGS AND STREAMERS

'With praises from children and from tiny infants, you have built a fortress.'
Psalm 8:2 CEV

YOU WILL NEED: scissors; paper; drinking straws; marker pen; glitter; sticky shapes; glue; crêpe paper; stapler; card.

It is often hard to find ways in which two- and three-year-olds can join in worship in a way that is appropriate to their age and capabilities. Their sheer joyful exuberance is a lesson to us all, so why not harness some of this energy and use it to praise God?

Write the words 'God is great!' or 'Praise God!' on one side of a small rectangle of paper. Fold the paper in half and stick it onto a drinking straw to make a simple flag. Help the children to decorate their flags with glitter and sticky shapes.

TOP TIP

Why not make the streamers in red, yellow and orange flame colours for the younger children to wave during a Pentecost praise service? For more lasting streamers use long ribbons instead of crêpe paper.

To make streamers, roll up a length of crêpe paper and cut a strip off the end about 2cm wide. Unroll the paper and you have one streamer. Put it together with two or three other colours. Fold over a small rectangle of card and staple the ends of the streamers inside to make a 'handle'. For extra safety place a square of sticky tape over the back of each staple to ensure that children don't hurt their fingers on the sharp ends.

Encourage the little ones to wave and twirl their flags or streamers while the rest of the congregation praise God with lively worship songs.

80. THREE IN ONE

'The grace of the Lord Jesus Christ, the love of God, and the fellowship of the Holy Spirit be with you all.'
2 Corinthians 13:13

YOU WILL NEED: a long strip of paper about 74cm long (try a broadsheet newspaper) and 9cm wide; scissors.

Show the group your strip of paper. Tape the two ends together to make a circle, but before you do this turn one end of the paper twice so that the circle has a twist in it. Explain that this circle represents God's never-ending love for us, and that the circle goes on and on just like God's love. God loved us so much that he sent his Son to tell us about him. God the Father and God the Son (Jesus) are different to each other but at the same time, both are completely God. Cut around your circle, about one third in from the edge, so that you make a second complete circle. When you have finished cutting the second circle, you will find that it is linked to the first circle although it is also a separate circle in its own right.

After Jesus had died for us, he came back to life and returned to his Father in heaven. God sent his Holy Spirit to help us and encourage us, to be our friend and helper. Take the thicker of the two circles and cut this in half so that you have a third circle also linked to the other two.

God the Holy Spirit is also a distinct person but is completely God at the same time. We call the Father, Son and Holy Spirit 'the Trinity', which means 'three in one'.

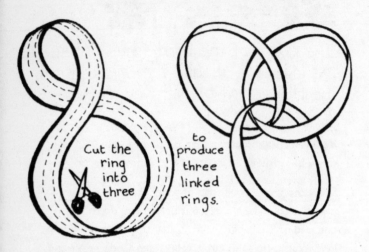

Cut the ring into three to produce three linked rings.

Invite the group to join in with the response *'We worship you!'* every time they hear the cue words, 'We want to tell you that…'.

God the Father, who designed and created our beautiful world, who formed and made us, we want to tell you that… *We worship you!*

God the Son, who walked on earth as a human being, who taught us about the Father's love, who died for our wrongdoing, we want to tell you that… *We worship you!*

God the Holy Spirit, who helps us and encourages us, who lives in us and enables us to live as Christians, we want to tell you that… *We worship you!*

PRAYERS FOR FESTIVALS AND SPECIAL DAYS

Special days deserve special prayers. A child who is nervous about going back to school needs to know that God knows and cares about how he feels. A child who is looking forward to her holiday with excitement and anticipation will be glad to know that God shares her joy.

At Christmas and Easter we decorate our church buildings and meeting rooms – why not include a prayer collage as part of the decoration? Paper chains and balloons, flowers and candles make the building look festive, but a prayer collage helps to focus the mind on what the festival is really about.

Many of the prayer suggestions that follow can be used with all ages together. In this way the children learn from the adults and vice versa. Never underestimate how much children can teach adults through their joyful, uninhibited and uncomplicated relationship with God.

81. NEW YEAR BLESSING

'Jesus Christ never changes! He is the same yesterday, today and for ever.'
Hebrews 13:8 CEV

YOU WILL NEED: small calendars; copies of prayer; card; glitter; sticky shapes; glue; hole punch; ribbon; sticky tape.

In advance, buy a number of the small calendars that are designed to hang under a photograph or painting. Give the youngsters a print-out of the prayer below and encourage them to colour an attractive border or stick glitter and shapes around the edge of the text. Paste the prayer onto a sheet of stiff card and punch two holes in the top so that you can thread a length of ribbon through to make a loop. Fix a calendar under each prayer and encourage the children to give this New Year Blessing to a special friend or relation.

In this coming year I pray that...

God's love will surround you,
God's wisdom will guide you,
God's word will teach you,
And God's ear will hear you.
Amen.

Calendar

82. VALENTINE'S DAY

'And God showed his love for us by sending his only Son into the world, so that we might have life through him.' I John 4:9

YOU WILL NEED: a Valentine's card; one large heart-shaped piece of paper; smaller hearts printed with the verse below; an envelope addressed to the group.

Make or buy a large Valentine's card and write the following words inside:

I love you so very much. In fact I sent my own Son into the world to show you just how much.

Your loving Father, God.

Cut out a large paper heart and glue it inside the card to make a pocket by sticking down the edges of the two long sides of the heart and leaving the top open. Fill the pocket with tiny heart-shapes printed with the words of I John 4:9.

Explain to your group that you have some special post addressed to the whole group. Open the envelope to reveal the Valentine's card. Talk about the fact that it's always fun wondering who the sender is and invite the group to guess. Open the card and read out the message. Explain that God doesn't want anyone to be in any doubt about just how much he loves them. This Valentine card is not anonymous and it is not just for one special person, but for every single person in the group because we are all very special to God. Take the small hearts out of the pocket inside the card and give one to each person. Explain that when we send Valentine's cards we always hope to receive one in return. God's greatest desire is that we will return his love. Display the words below and invite everone to join in with the response in italics. Display the words below and invite everyone to join in with the response in italics.

Father God you created us and made us your own.

Thank-you for loving us.

You sent your own Son to tell us just how much you care.

Thank-you for loving us.

You gave the life of Jesus so that we might live.

Thank-you for loving us.

You go on and on loving us even when we don't deserve it.

Thank-you for loving us.

Help us to return your love.

Amen.

83. HOT CROSS BUNS

'Then they put him to death by nailing him to a cross.' Acts 10:39

YOU WILL NEED: enough hot cross buns for everyone to try a piece; butter (optional); plate.

Hold up a hot cross bun and ask the group if they know why we eat these buns at Easter. Say that millions of people in many different countries eat hot cross buns to remember how Jesus suffered on the cross for our wrongdoing.

Think about some of the ingredients needed to make the buns. Yeast is needed to make the buns rise; it can also remind us that Jesus did not stay dead – he rose again. Dried fruits are added to the mixture; these remind us of the good things that come from Jesus' death. Without his death on the cross we would not be able to enjoy new life.

Pass round the hot cross buns and, in a time of quiet, invite everyone to take a piece and eat it. As the group does this encourage everyone to take this opportunity to silently thank Jesus in their heart for his willingness to die a slow and painful death so that we might live.

84. LIGHT TRIUMPHS

'The light shines in the darkness, and the darkness has never put it out.'
John 1:5

YOU WILL NEED: a relighting candle (test it at home first); a box of matches.

Dim the lights and sit in a circle around the lit candle. Explain that Jesus was the light of the world and say that when he died, the devil thought that he had put out the light. Blow the candle out. As it relights, explain that Jesus' power was greater than the darkness, and he came back to life. Use the following prayer with your group, inviting everyone to join in with the response in italics.

Thank-you, Jesus, for your love for us.
Hallelujah! Jesus is the king!
Thank-you for suffering so that we can have new life.
Hallelujah! Jesus is the king!
We praise you because you defeated death.
Hallelujah! Jesus is the king!
Help us to know that you are always close to us.
Hallelujah! Jesus is the king!

(With thanks to Nicola Perryman.)

This idea can easily be adapted for use at alternative hallowe'en celebrations.

85. FLORAL CROSS

'The Lord is risen indeed!' Luke 24:34

YOU WILL NEED: large piece of brown cardboard; flower shapes cut from brightly coloured paper; pens; glue.

In advance cut an enormous cross out of cardboard (if possible, use corrugated card to give a textured effect). Talk about how the cross reminds us of the events of Good Friday. In fact Good Friday was not a good day at all, but a very sad day on which we remember that Jesus was put to death on the cross even though he had done nothing wrong. Some people think that the name Good Friday may have derived from 'God's Friday', just as 'goodbye' comes from 'God be with ye'. Others believe that we call the day Good Friday because in the old days the word 'good' was often used to mean 'holy'. In many European languages Good Friday is called 'Great Friday'. On Good Friday Jesus certainly did a very great thing for all mankind. He gave his life for our wrongdoing, so that all who believe in him might be free.

The cross is a symbol of Jesus' death, but Jesus did not stay on the cross: he rose again, and so it is also a symbol of our new life in him. Give out the flower shapes and invite everyone to write a short prayer on their flower thanking Jesus for his amazing love. Young children could draw a happy face. Play some rousing Easter music and invite everyone to come up and stick their flower prayers onto the cross.

TOP TIP
In a family service get children to collect the flowers and stick them onto the cross during a joyful Easter hymn.

86. MOTHERING SUNDAY

'I will comfort you there like a mother comforting her child.' Isaiah 66:13 CEV

YOU WILL NEED: selection of props as listed opposite.

Say that mums play many different and important roles in family life. Pull out your props one at a time and talk about some of the tasks that mums carry out.

For example:

Whisk: they cook for us.
Bandage: they look after us when we're injured.
Cough medicine: they nurse us when we're ill.
Car keys: they take us to places (to school, to church, to see our friends) and bring us safely back home again.
Washing powder: they wash and iron our clothes.
Screwdriver: they fix things.
Storybook: they tell us bedtime stories.
Exercise book: they help us with homework.
A big paper heart: they go on and on loving us, even when we're naughty.

Give out the props to a number of different children and ask them to each say a one-line prayer thanking God that mums do that particular thing for us. Alternatively, say a concluding thank-you prayer yourself, weaving in all the different roles mentioned.

Adapt this idea for use on Father's Day, remembering that we enjoy the privilege of having two fathers, one on earth and one in heaven.

87. PENTECOST FLAMES

'Then they saw what looked like tongues of fire which spread out and touched each person there.' Acts 2:3

YOU WILL NEED: orange, red and yellow coloured paper; scissors; pencils; glue; black backing paper.

Explain to your group that when the Holy Spirit first arrived it looked as if flames of fire were reaching out and touching people. This was not the kind of fire that burnt people, but flames which filled everyone present with the warmth of God's love and fired up their hearts with courage and enthusiasm.

God sent his Holy Spirit to help all that believe in him to live as Christians. The Holy Spirit can still help people today to praise and pray, to read and understand the Bible and to share their faith with others. The Spirit lives in us as our own special helper.

Give out sheets of red, yellow or orange paper and encourage everyone to draw around their hand and cut it out. They can then write a short prayer thanking God for the gift of his special helper. When everyone has finished, stick the hands onto black background paper to make them look like one huge flame.

88. OFF ON HOLIDAY

'You let me rest in fields of green grass. You lead me to streams of peaceful water, and you refresh my life.' Psalm 23:2,3 CEV

YOU WILL NEED: a suitcase packed with props listed below.

At the end of the summer term, you might like to pray

for people who are preparing to go on holiday. Bring in a suitcase in which you have put one or two props that will remind you of different areas to pray about. Unpack the suitcase and hold up the items one at a time. Ask the children to suggest what each thing reminds us to pray for. Finally, ask a leader to weave all their suggestions into one prayer, or give out the props and ask a number of youngsters to contribute to the prayer.

You might like to include some of the following items:

Passport: pray for those going abroad, thank God for the enjoyment of meeting people from other countries, ask for help in understanding other languages.

Sun cream: pray for good weather and for safety in the sun.

Map: pray for safe travel and for help in finding the best route.

Bucket and spade, swimming costume, ball: thank God for all the different activities that may be enjoyed while on holiday.

Pillow: pray for rest and relaxation for those who really need a holiday.

Postcard: pray for any loved ones who will be left behind.

First aid box: pray for safety and good health throughout the holiday.

89. PRAYER POSTCARD

'Give thanks to the Lord, because he is good; his love is eternal.' Psalm 136:1

YOU WILL NEED: two or three postcards; sticky address labels; a large sheet of paper ruled to look like a postcard, addressed to God and with a pretend stamp.

Show the group one or two postcards that you received during the holidays and read out any appropriate messages. Talk about how pleased you felt that friends remembered you when they were away. When we're on holiday our routine is different and sometimes we forget to pray. Give everyone a sticky address label and invite them to write a short prayer message to God. They might want to thank him for a holiday they have enjoyed, for a safe journey and good weather. They might want to thank him for the chance to relax at home and see friends, or to praise him for all the beautiful places and scenery that the holiday has given them the time to enjoy. Younger children might prefer to draw a place or activity that they have enjoyed while on holiday.

Invite the children to collect up all the labels and stick them on the postcard while the group sings an appropriate worship song. Finish by thanking God for all the good things about holidays and including some of the messages on the postcard.

90. BACK TO SCHOOL

'Pay attention to your teacher and
learn all you can.' Proverbs 23:12

YOU WILL NEED: a school bag packed with props listed
below.

This is a prayer to use at the end of August when we
think about children starting infant or secondary school
for the first time or returning to school after the summer
holidays. Bring in a school bag in which you have put
several props that will remind you about different areas
to pray about. As you take them out of the bag, one by
one, ask the children to suggest what each prop reminds
us of. Then, if your group is happy to pray aloud give out
the props and ask different children to pray for that
aspect of school life. Alternatively, hold up the props
yourself and pray that your group will enjoy their return
to school.

You might like to include some of the following:

An exercise book: pray that the youngsters will be
ready to work hard and that they will find the subjects
interesting and enjoyable.

A tennis ball: pray for happy lunchtimes and playtimes,
for good friends to play with and talk to. Pray that those
starting at new schools will quickly make new friends.

A red pen: pray for kind, understanding teachers who can explain things well and enable the class to enjoy learning new things. Pray for children who will meet a new teacher this term and for Christian teachers in your congregation.

A pair of shoes: pray for safe travelling as children walk, cycle or are driven to school. Thank God for the lollipop men and women who help us to cross the road safely.

Bible: Thank God that wherever we are, at home or at school, he is always with us. Read one or two verses from Psalm 139:7–12. Pray that God will provide teachers and friends who share our Christian beliefs.

91. HARVEST FRUIT BASKET

'What a rich harvest your goodness provides!' Psalm 65:11

YOU WILL NEED: a simple outline of a basket glued onto backing paper; paper fruit shapes; pens; glue.

Use coloured paper to cut out a number of simple fruit shapes: apples, bananas, pears, grapes, oranges, etc. With very young children you might like to place the shapes onto an OHP and let them guess each fruit by its silhouette. Include a few more difficult shapes to challenge the older children, eg mango, kiwi or passion fruit. If you have time, cut up some of the exotic fruit and let the children sample them, then ask them to compare flavours and textures and to decide on their favourite fruit. Finally, give out the fruit shapes and ask everyone to write or draw a one-line prayer thanking God for their favourite fruit. Paste all the finished fruit shapes inside the outline of a basket. Conclude by offering the whole basket to God with a special prayer thanking him for the wonderful harvest that he provides.

92. SOWING GOD'S WORD

'Those seeds that fell on good ground are the people who listen to the message and keep it in good and honest hearts. They last and produce a harvest.' Luke 8:15 CEV

YOU WILL NEED: paper seed-shapes; paper circles; glue; backing paper; pens.

Read Luke 8:4–15 and then point out that if we have heard and understood God's Word and if God's love is growing in our lives then it is good to sow a seed by passing this on to others. Give everyone a seed-shape and invite them to write a one-line prayer asking God to help them tell someone else about Jesus. Younger children could draw people that they'd like to introduce to Jesus. Glue the finished 'seed' prayers onto backing paper around coloured paper circles so that they look like fully grown sunflowers. Use a green marker pen to add stalks and leaves (see illustration overpage). Finish with a concluding prayer asking God to help the whole group to share the seeds of their faith with others so that a wonderful harvest is sown.

93. LIVING WORD (BIBLE SUNDAY)

 3-5    6-11

'The word of God is alive and active...'
Hebrews 4:12

YOU WILL NEED: a box with a lid; shredded newspaper; a Bible.

In advance, place a Bible inside a box under a layer of shredded newspaper. Make some air holes in the top of the box and write THIS WAY UP in large letters on the front. The aim, of course, is to make the group think that you have a small pet inside.

Bring out the box from its hiding place and explain to your group that you have brought along something living to show them today. You can get them in several colours, eg black, brown or white. This one is very special to you and you've had it for quite a long time. It's with you every day and has become a special friend. You enjoy spending time with it and believe that it helps you to enjoy life more. Peer inside the box and remove some of the shredded paper with lots of comments like 'Where are you? I know that you're in here somewhere? Out you come!' Finally show your group the Bible!

Explain that, in many ways, the Bible is just as much alive as a rabbit or a guinea pig! It is a living book, which has outlived many generations of people and their pets. The Bible says that God's Word is 'living and eternal' (see 1 Peter 1:23), and it is full of advice and encouragement, which is just as relevant today as it was yesterday and will be tomorrow. The Bible tells us the true story of God's people and of his Son Jesus. It teaches us how to live today and how to claim God's gift of eternal life. Display the following words to say as a group:

Lord God,
Thank-you for your living Word, the Bible.
Thank-you for the advice and encouragement it contains.
Help me to read and understand your special book,
so that your Word will live in my heart.
Amen.

(With thanks to Antony Wareham.)

94. GOD'S SWORD (BIBLE SUNDAY)

'Let God's saving power be like a helmet, and for a sword use God's message that comes from the Spirit.' Ephesians 6:17 CEV

YOU WILL NEED: one rectangle of silver foil per person.

Give everyone a piece of silver foil and allow a couple of minutes for them to fold, scrunch or model it into a sword. Talk about how a sword can be used to attack things that are bad and also to ward off unwelcome attacks. Jesus used his knowledge of the Scriptures like a sword to defeat the devil (see Matthew 4:1–11).

Point out that a sword isn't much use unless it is in your hand; equally the Bible isn't any use to us unless we open and read it.

Pray, thanking God for his special book and asking that he will help the whole group to read, remember and understand his Word.

95. WILL YOU OPEN THE DOOR? (BIBLE SUNDAY)

'All Scripture is inspired by God.'
2 Timothy 3:16

YOU WILL NEED: a large Bible with an illustration of a door stuck on the front cover.

Explain to your group that in many ways the Bible is like a door; a door that we pass every day. It has a handle on it and we can open the door and go in whenever we like, but many people are just too busy. They pass the door every day, but they never go in. They are missing the opportunity of meeting all kinds of wonderful people. If we open the door we will meet many famous people like Noah, Moses and Daniel. If we open the door we will be able to meet Jesus and get to know him better.

Ask the group to help you make a list of some of the different types of writing in the Bible: letters, poems, stories about Jesus, history, rules, good news, etc. Weave all of their suggestions into a simple response prayer, such as the following:

Lord, thank-you for your special book, the Bible,

Help us to read and remember your Word.

Thank-you for the stories it contains,

Help us to read and remember your Word.

Thank-you for the letters that give us encouragement

Help us to read and remember your Word.

Thank-you for the rules that teach us how to live.

Help us to read and remember your Word

Thank-you for the good news that gives us a certain hope for the future.

Help us to read and remember your Word

etc.

96. CHRISTMAS STOCKING

'Then the ones who pleased the Lord will ask, " When did we give you something to eat or drink? When did we welcome you as a stranger or give you clothes to wear or visit you while you were sick or in jail?" The King will answer, "Whenever you did it for any of my people, no matter how unimportant they seemed, you did it for me."' Matthew 25:37-40 CEV

YOU WILL NEED: backing paper; tinsel; paper Christmas stocking shape; parcel shapes cut from gift-wrap; ribbons; glue.

At Christmas it is easy to exchange cards and gifts with each other and forget the person whose birthday it really is. Can you imagine how you'd feel if it was your birthday, and everyone else received a present but you? Cut out a large Christmas stocking shape from red paper and trim the top with tinsel. Then, cut some parcel shapes out of gift-wrap and glue the stocking with the parcels spilling out of the top onto backing paper. Add a few ribbons to the parcels to make them look extra festive. Explain that this stocking is a gift for Jesus.

Give out large sticky address labels and ask the group to write or draw something that they might like to give to Jesus. Of course, we can't give Jesus anything face to face, but Jesus said that anything that we do for someone in need we do for him (see verse above). Ask the group to think about whether they could give a little of their time, money, talents or prayers to help someone else. They should then write their ideas on their labels and stick them onto the parcels as a gift for Jesus. For example: I'll take some mince pies to my elderly neighbour; I'll give some of my pocket money to the NSPCC; I'll give the toys that I've outgrown to a charity shop; I'll pack up a box for the shoe-box appeal.

When all the labels have been stuck onto the Christmas stocking, finish with a prayer offering the collage and all the promises to Jesus.

97. CHRISTMAS THOUGHT

'So they hurried off and found Mary and Joseph and saw the baby lying in the manger.' Luke 2:16

At Christmas we send **C**ards to each other
And hang sprigs of **h**olly around picture frames.
We hum Rudolph the **r**ed nosed reindeer
As we put **i**vy into floral decorations.
Children write a list for **S**anta
And help drape **t**insel on the tree.
Mum makes scores of **m**ince pies
And little girls look **a**ngelic in nativity plays.
But don't forget the **S**on of God, for it's his birthday
that we're celebrating, **T**hough …
an outs**i**der
might be forgiven
for not r**e**alising.

98. CHRISTINGLES

'I have come into the world as light, so that everyone who believes in me should not remain in the darkness.'
John 12:46

YOU WILL NEED: oranges; red ribbon; cocktail sticks; sweets and dried fruit; birthday cake candles and holders.

Although the Christingle has been around for many years, for many people in this country they are, in fact, a new idea. The Christingle service (meaning Christ light or Christ child), in which decorated oranges are distributed, began over 250 years ago in a Moravian church in Marienborn, Germany. This tradition has spread around the world and many churches in the UK now hold an annual Christingle service in aid of The Children's Society (see www.the-childrens-society.org.uk).

During the service each child receives a Christingle, which is an orange (representing the world) with a red ribbon tied around it (representing Christ's blood shed for the world). A small candle is stuck into the top of the orange (use a birthday cake candle and holder) to represent Jesus, the light of the world. Four cocktail sticks, spiked with dried fruits or small sweets, are stuck into the sides of the orange to represent the people of the world and the sweetness of knowing Jesus. The

Christingle service is more than just a candlelit service, since each orange tells the story of Jesus' love for the world.

Lord Jesus,
You are the light, which shines in the darkness.
You are the light, which guides our feet.
You are the light, which fills us with a warm glow.
You are the light, which illuminates our lives.
You are the light, which leads us to safety.
You are the light, which will shine forever.
You are the light of the world and we worship you.
Amen.

99. AN ARMY OF ANGELS

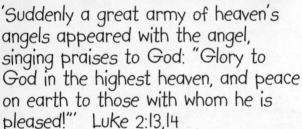

'Suddenly a great army of heaven's angels appeared with the angel, singing praises to God: "Glory to God in the highest heaven, and peace on earth to those with whom he is pleased!"' Luke 2:13,14

YOU WILL NEED: dark backing paper; angel pictures; glue; pens; glitter; sticky stars.

Tell your group the wonderful story of how the angels appeared to the shepherds in the field one dark night (Luke 2:8–20). With a young group, you might like to use a version from a Children's Bible.

Give everyone a copy of the angel picture (see illustration) and ask them to write their own short prayer on the angel's robe thanking God for the gift of his Son at Christmas. Anyone who is unsure what to write might consider copying the angel's words from Luke 2:14. Young children could colour in their angel picture in bright colours.

Play some Christmas music while the group glues all the prayers onto the backing paper to look like an army or a host of angels. Alternatively, ask a few young volunteers to help you complete the collage while the adults sing some appropriate Christmas carols. As a finishing touch add a sprinkling of glitter and sticky stars to the backing paper.

100. GIFT-SHAPED PRAYERS

'...pray always for all God's people.'
Ephesians 6:18

YOU WILL NEED: a large outline of a Christmas tree; tinsel; squares and rectangles of coloured paper or large sticky labels.

Take a moment to stop and think about those people for whom Christmas will not be happy this year. These could include people who have been recently bereaved, those in war-torn countries, the homeless, those who are ill, those

who have lost their jobs recently. All of these needy people deserve a special Christmas present and, even though we don't know many of these people personally, we can still give them the gift of our prayers. Give out the squares and rectangles of paper, or the sticky labels, and invite the group to write their own prayers for those in need this Christmas. Stick all the prayer-presents onto the outline of the Christmas tree. Decorate the tree with tinsel and then offer all the gifts to God in a concluding prayer.

101. HOLLY WREATH

'She gave birth to her first son, wrapped him in strips of cloth and laid him in a manger – there was no room for them to stay in the inn.' Luke 2:7

YOU WILL NEED: holly leaves cut from green paper; a large ring of card; small red circles; pens; glue.

Many people hang a welcoming wreath on their door at Christmas time, so why not make a similar wreath to hang on the door of your church or meeting room? When Jesus was born, he didn't receive a warm welcome inside the inn because there was no room there. His expectant mother was sent to give birth in a stable round the back! Make a point of welcoming Jesus to your Christmas celebrations this year.

Give out the paper holly leaves and ask the group to write short prayers on them, inviting Jesus to be a part of their Christmas celebrations, or thanking God for his special gift. Suggest that young children draw a picture of themselves with their arms open in welcome. Stick all the prayers onto the circle of card and add a few red paper berries. Attach a ribbon and hang the prayer collage on your door. Finish by reading out some of the prayers and dedicating the wreath to God.

INDEX OF TITLES

PRAYERS TO JOIN IN

PRAYERS TO WRITE, DRAW AND MAKE

PRAYERS FOR FESTIVALS AND SPECIAL DAYS

With thanks to the writers
of SALT 8 to 10+
whose hard work and creativity is a
constant source of inspiration.

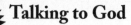

Talking to God

Margaret Barfield, illustrated by Branwen Thomas

A lively book of prayers to encourage 4-6 year olds to talk openly to God about themselves, their feelings and everyday life. Illustrations in colour and black and white add to the appeal.

1 85999 166 1
£3.99

Hello God It's Me

Stephanie King, illustrated by Helen Mahood

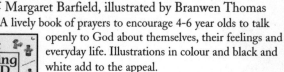

A collection of refreshingly original prayers to help children learn to talk to God about everyday life. 8 short sections, enhanced with illustrations, cover child-friendly topics such as: my family, learning, travelling, playing, special times.

1 85999 462 8
£3.99

Multi-Sensory Prayer: Over 60 innovative ready-to-use ideas

Sue Wallace

A tried and tested collection of fresh ideas to help young people meet God in active, experiential prayer. Hands-on, step by step tips on everything from innovative new techniques to meditations and rituals borrowed from across the Christian tradition. Ideal for youth groups, small groups and church services.

A photocopiable resource
1 95999 465 2
A4 £7.99

Here's One I Made Earlier

Craft resources for childrens leaders

Compiled by Kathryn Copsey
A wealth of tried and tested craft ideas for use with 3-11 year olds. Includes chapters on pictures, puppets, mobiles, banners, models, and many more, which are linked to Bible stories.
'Packed with lots of ideas, good value and should keep you going for a while!'
Children's Ministry
0 86201 981 8
A4 £6.99

Here's Another One I Made Earlier

Compiled by Christine Orme
More exciting craft ideas for use with your children's groups, arranged thematically for easy reference. Subjects cover Advent, Christmas, Mothering Sunday, Easter, Prayer, God's world and many more.
1 85999 338 9
A4 £7.99

You can obtain any of these books from:

- ◆ Your local Christian bookshop
- ◆ Scripture Union Mail Order: Phone our Subscriptions and Mail Order Department on 01908 856006.
- ◆ Online: Log on to www.scriptureunion.org.uk/publishing to order securely from our online bookshop.

Prices are correct at time of going to print.